1992

CHEROKEE REMOVAL
Before and After

CHEROKEE REMOVAL
Before and After

EDITED BY

William L. Anderson

THE UNIVERSITY OF GEORGIA PRESS

Athens and London

© 1991 by the University of Georgia Press
Athens, Georgia 30602
All rights reserved
Designed by Betty Palmer McDaniel
Set in Galliard with Bodoni Open display
The paper in this book meets the guidelines for permanence
and durability of the Committee on Production Guidelines for
Book Longevity of the Council on Library Resources.

Printed in the United States of America

95 94 93 92 91   5 4 3 2 1

Library of Congress Cataloging in Publication Data

Cherokee removal : before and after / edited by
William L. Anderson.
p. cm.
Includes bibliographical references.
Includes index.
ISBN 0-8203-1254-1 (alk. paper).
1. Cherokee Indians—Removal.   2. Cherokee Indians—
History.
I. Anderson, William L., date.
E99.C5C6523 1991
973'.04975—dc20   90-36731
CIP

British Library Cataloging in Publication Data available

Chapter three was originally published as "The Conflict Within: The Cherokee Power Structure and Removal," *The Georgia Historical Quarterly* 73 (Fall 1989): 467–91, published by the Georgia Historical Society, Savannah, in cooperation with the Franklin College of Arts and Sciences, the Institute of Higher Education and the department of History, the University of Georgia, Athens. © 1989 by the Georgia Historical Society and reprinted with permission.

The maps on pages 82 and 119 are reprinted by permission, from Mary E. Rogers, *A Brief History of the Cherokees* (Baltimore: Gateway Press, 1986), © Mary E. Rogers. Adapted from Grace S. Woodward, *The Cherokees* (Norman: University of Oklahoma Press, 1963).

The ornaments used in this book are Cherokee designs featured on Pisgah pottery (ca. A.D. 1000–1450), from *Cherokee Prehistory* by Roy S. Dickens, Jr., published by The University of Tennessee Press, 1976.

Contents

CONTENTS

Introduction

WILLIAM L. ANDERSON

The removal of the Cherokee Nation from its homeland in the Southeast to a new territory beyond the Mississippi remains a compelling and controversial event in United States history. The Cherokees were only one of many native peoples forcibly relocated in the first half of the nineteenth century, but for their contemporaries and subsequent generations, Cherokee removal has assumed a particular drama and poignancy. The Cherokees, more than any other native people, tried to adopt Anglo-American culture. In a remarkably short time, they transformed their society and modified their traditional culture in order to conform to United States policy, to fulfill the expectations of white politicians and philanthropists, and most important, to preserve their tribal integrity. On the eve of Cherokee removal to the West, many white Americans considered them to be the most "civilized" of all native peoples. How then did the Cherokees come to be removed? Why were they forced to abandon homes, farms, schools, and churches? What terrible chain of events culminated in this catastrophe?

Almost since contact, whites had been removing Indians from land whites wanted. When the Cherokees first encountered Europeans, the Cherokee Nation claimed an area spanning what would eventually become eight states and encompassing more than 124,000 square miles. Beginning in 1721 the Cherokees made a number of "voluntary" land cessions, and the American Revolution triggered a series of forced cessions. By the end of the Revolution in 1783 Cherokee territory had been reduced by almost 60 percent (70,000 square miles). The new American government continued to seek land cessions as it pushed west, and from 1783 to 1819 the Cherokees lost an additional 69 percent of their remaining land. By 1819 they held only 17,000 square miles of the original 124,000.[1]

The United States policy that resulted in Cherokee removal evolved gradually. In the early years of the Republic, seizure of Indian land gave way to a policy of "civilizing" native Americans. First articulated by George Washington's secretary of war, Henry Knox, this policy aimed at transforming the wandering hunter who owned land communally, governed himself by barbaric custom, worshipped spirits, and spoke a "savage" language into a sedentary farmer who owned land individually, governed himself by written law, worshipped the one true god, and spoke English learned in proper schools. This policy, of course, rested on an ethnocentric and inaccurate view of native culture, but facts have never figured prominently in the development of United States Indian policy. The Indians had to give up "only" their hunting, language, religion, tribal organizations, and customs. After all, making civilized men out of "savages" would benefit the Indians and the new nation as well as ensure the progress of the human race.[2] On the surface, the original goal of the "civilizing" policy seemed generous and philanthropic; beneath the surface, however, the policy represented a new attempt to wrest the Indians' land from them. Knox and his successors reasoned that if Indians gave up hunting, their hunting grounds would become "surplus" land that they would willingly exchange for funds to support education, agriculture, and other "civilized" pursuits. According to this reasoning, coercing the Indians to cede their hunting grounds would actually accelerate acculturation because they could no longer dawdle in the forest when they had fields to till. The architects of this policy did not foresee one possible result—acculturation might make native peoples even more determined to hold on to their domain and more capable of resisting United States demands. This, of course, was precisely the consequence of the "civilization" policy for the Cherokees who enthusiastically embraced its tenets.[3]

The "civilization" policy required an almost total reorganization of the spiritual, social, and psychological world of the Cherokees. Yet by adopting white culture, the Cherokees hoped to gain white respect. Acculturation, then, was partly a defensive mechanism to prevent further loss of land and extinction of native culture, the very goals whites saw as the objective of acculturation. On the other hand, many Cherokees firmly believed that "civilization" was preferable to their traditional way of life. Whatever the reason, some Cherokees adopted much Anglo-American culture. They established schools, developed written laws, and abolished clan revenge. Cherokee women became involved in spinning and weaving while men raised livestock and planted crops. The progress of the Cherokees astounded many whites who traveled through their country in the early nineteenth century. Some Cherokees even built columned plantation houses and bought scores of slaves. Christianity also made inroads among the Cherokees with the appearance of missionaries from five different Protestant denominations.[4]

Several clouds appeared to threaten Cherokee progress. The Louisiana Purchase in 1803 provided whites with an immediate alternative to "civilization" and assimilation of the Indians—removal. When the "civilization" program failed to transform the Indians overnight, the philanthropists who had supported it agreed that the "savages" should not be permitted to remain in the midst of a civilized society. The only solution, short of the complete extermination advocated by some frontiersmen, was removal to the West.[5]

Several other factors contributed to the fate of the Cherokees, among them the discovery of gold on Cherokee land, the issue of states' rights, and the emergence of scientific racism. The invention of the cotton gin also created in the white man an even greater desire for agricultural land, and finally, the Creek War of 1813–14 ended any possible threat of an Indian confederation against the whites.

In 1817 the United States government negotiated the first Cherokee treaty that included a provision for removal. This 1817 treaty proposed exchanging Cherokee land in the Southeast for territory west of the Mississippi. The government promised assistance in resettling in the West to those Cherokees who chose to remove.[6] Approximately 1,500 to 2,000 Cherokees elected to go west despite the intense opposition of Cherokee leaders and the clear preference of the majority for remaining in the East. These emigrants joined Cherokees who had drifted west at the turn of the century and those who had chosen to migrate under United States auspices in 1808–10.[7] In fact, it was the presence of these Cherokees on federal lands in the West that in part prompted United States demands for Chero-kee cessions in 1817. The treaty of 1817 also contained a proposal for an experiment in citizenship. Cherokees who wished to remain on ceded land in the East could apply for a 640-acre reserve and citizenship. However, the federal government was slow to survey some of the land designated as Indian reserves and underestimated the states' rights movement, the claims of revolutionary war veterans, and the overall white greed for land. Had the states supported this experiment it might have achieved Indian assimilation. Instead, the southern states fought it, even using legal techni-calities to render Indian claims invalid. Here perhaps the whites were not solely to blame for the failure of the experiment. Most of the Cherokees did not support the 1817 treaty, and the Cherokee Council voted in 1819 to deny citizenship in the tribe to anyone who emigrated west or accepted a reserve. Among the Cherokees who elected to receive reservations were those along the Oconaluftee River in North Carolina.[8] This decision sev-ered their legal relations with the Cherokee Nation. Consequently, when the United States implemented the 1835 removal treaty with the Cherokee Nation these people were exempt from the treaty's provisions. They and their descendants remained in North Carolina.

The Cherokees who opposed removal also sought and obtained another treaty in 1819, which enabled them to maintain communal ownership of more than ten million acres of their ancestral lands in the East. Although the Cherokees ceded almost four million acres by that treaty, they hoped that this additional cession would end any removal effort. Indeed, the Cherokee Nation in the East would not negotiate another cession; refusal to do so led the United States to turn to an unauthorized faction for the final cession.[9]

At about the same time the Cherokees accelerated their acculturation. They increased the number of written laws and established a bicameral legislature. In the early 1820s a Cherokee named Sequoyah invented a syl-labary that enabled the Cherokees to read and write in their own language, and the Cherokees soon established a newspaper printed in both English and Cherokee that espoused acculturation and opposition to removal. By 1827 the Cherokees had also established a supreme court and a constitution very similar to those of the United States. The signs of Cherokee achieve-ment were everywhere: their new capital with its handsome buildings at

New Echota; their well-dressed forceful leaders; their new gristmills, sawmills, and turnpikes; and their educated young men, who provided proof
that a Cherokee could do everything a white man could do. Some of these
scholars had attended the American Board's seminary in Cornwall, Connecticut, and could read Latin and Greek as well as understand the white
man's philosophy, history, theology, and politics.[10]

Without a doubt the Cherokees more than met the goals proposed for
the Indians by various United States presidents from George Washington
to Andrew Jackson. In the words of one Cherokee scholar, the Cherokees
were the "mirror of the American Republic."[11] But in the period after
1820 the future of the Cherokees and other native Americans was seriously
jeopardized as white Americans began to embrace a belief in white superiority and the static nature of the "red man." Many Americans concluded,
"once an Indian, always an Indian." Culture, they believed, was innate,
not learned. However "civilized" an Indian might appear, he retained a
"savage" nature.[12]

Another factor vital to the issue of removal was states' rights. Although
the Cherokees saw their constitution as a crowning achievement, whites,
especially Georgians, viewed it as a challenge to states' rights, because
they believed that Cherokee territory was within the boundaries of four
states. Georgians were already upset that the federal government seemed
to be procrastinating in fulfilling the compact of 1802. By this compact
Georgia had relinquished its claim to western lands in return for a federal government promise to extinguish Indian titles to all lands within the
state. Georgians viewed the treaties of 1817 and 1819 as lost opportunities
to implement the compact. They were even more annoyed in 1823 when
President James Monroe seemed to interpret the compact of 1802 as giving
the Cherokees the right to refuse any more land cessions and in 1825 when
President John Quincy Adams refused to accept a treaty negotiated by
only a faction of the Creeks.[13] The 1827 Cherokee Constitution claimed
sovereignty over tribal lands, establishing a state within a state. Georgians
claimed that such a legal maneuver violated the United States Constitution and that the federal government was doing nothing to remedy the
situation.

President Andrew Jackson, however, in his first annual message to Congress, recognized state control over local Indians, repudiated recent Chero-

kee claims to sovereignty, and called upon Congress to provide an act for Indian removal. Less than two weeks later, Georgia, assured of presidential sympathy, passed a series of laws that abolished Cherokee government, began the enforcement of state law in Indian country, and authorized a survey of Cherokee land that was to be distributed by lottery to Georgia citizens. Unable to get support from the president or Congress, the Cherokees took their case to the Supreme Court. In the famous *Worcester v. Georgia* decision, Chief Justice John Marshall declared that Georgia had exceeded its authority by extending state law into Cherokee territory. Georgia refused to recognize Supreme Court jurisdiction over the state, leaving Jackson legally powerless. Federal marshals could not be sent to enforce the law until a state judge refused to comply with the Supreme Court decision, and Georgia chose to ignore the court's decision rather than challenge it. The legal opportunity to enforce the decision never arose.[14] Had Jackson been inclined to intervene he could well have driven Georgia and the other southern states onto the side of South Carolina in that state's controversy over the nullification of federal tariffs. Even Jackson's opponents realized the danger to the Union in the Worcester decision, and they tempered accordingly their criticism of the president.[15] In the end, unionist sympathy proved greater than sympathy for the Cherokees. Even devoted supporters of the Cherokee cause began to urge the tribe to sign a removal treaty. In one sense, the Cherokees were sacrificed to keep the Union together.

By 1833 a minority party developed within the Cherokee Nation, led by Major Ridge, a hero of the War of 1812, his New England–educated son John Ridge, and Elias Boudinot, former editor of the *Cherokee Phoenix*. These men believed removal was inevitable, and they sought a treaty on the best possible terms. The majority of the Cherokees (almost 16,000), led by Chief John Ross, opposed removal. Ignoring the majority, United States commissioners negotiated the fraudulent Treaty of New Echota in 1835 with a handful of unauthorized individuals. In spite of a petition from over 15,000 Cherokees protesting the treaty, the United States Senate ratified the Treaty of New Echota in May 1836. The Cherokees were given two years to emigrate west to Indian territory or face forced removal. By 1838 only 2,000 of the 16,000 had moved west, and the government sent in seven thousand militia and volunteers to remove those remaining. The

Introduction

Cherokees were rounded up at bayonet point and herded into stockades. The Indians were allowed little or no time to gather possessions. As they turned for one last glimpse of their homes, they often saw them being ransacked for valuables by whites or put to the torch. The first detachment of Cherokees departed from Tennessee in June 1838. Resigned to their inevitable deportation, Chief John Ross then prevailed upon the Van Buren administration to permit the Cherokees to remove themselves. Inadequate food, extreme cold, and disease were among the factors resulting in extremely high losses of life for the Cherokee Nation.

Uprooted from their homeland, the Cherokees arrived at the new territory in a state of shock. Few families escaped the death of a relative. Factionalism and civil war erupted, ending, at least on paper, in 1846. The coming of the American Civil War brought a reemergence of the factionalism, which was still operative during Reconstruction. Whites continued to interfere with tribal government and Indian society, culminating at the end of the century in the dissolution of tribal government. The Curtis Act of 1898 brought the breakup of communally held tribal lands through individual allotments. Once again the goal was to "civilize" the Indians and force them into the mainstream of society. Corruption and greed soon subverted whatever philanthropy might have originally motivated policy makers, and as with removal, many Cherokees suffered. Under the Indian Reorganization Act of 1934, Cherokees and other native peoples gained some control over their own affairs, but the legacy of removal endured. Two Cherokee Nations—one in North Carolina and one in Oklahoma— are reminders of that era.

The year 1988 marked the 150th anniversary of the Trail of Tears, which this volume commemorates. The scholarly analyses of the period immediately before and after Cherokee removal represent the first broad interdisciplinary approach in the study of removal. The contributors include several historians, a geographer, a sociologist, and a lawyer; three of the seven contributors are of Cherokee ancestry.

Douglas C. Wilms, a geographer, uses Cherokee censuses, Cherokee property valuations, and more than 55,000 plats to determine the use of land by the Cherokees in Georgia prior to their expulsion in 1838. His information, supported by ample maps and charts, serves as further proof of the extent of Cherokee acculturation. If Cherokee land-use patterns had been widely known and appreciated during the debate over the removal bill, the Cherokees might have found more congressional allies.

Historian Ronald N. Satz discusses the dangers of oversimplified, one-dimensional interpretations of Jacksonian Indian policy. He shows how despite the rhetoric of Jacksonian policy, which emphasized its philanthropic goals, neither Jackson nor his administration was willing to undertake the necessary planning to ensure the fruition of these goals. Satz argues that the vast contrast between the rhetoric and the reality of Jacksonian Indian policy serves as a grim reminder of what can happen to a politically powerless minority in a democratic society.

Historian Theda Perdue critically examines the Cherokee political system and class structure. She challenges traditional viewpoints on the motives of those who signed the treaty ceding the remaining Cherokee land east of the Mississippi. Perdue sees the internal dissension among the Cherokees before removal as a class struggle between a Cherokee elite and a rising Cherokee middle class. It was the inability of the Cherokee middle class to achieve its political and economic goals, and not strong pro-removal sentiment, that led them to negotiate the Treaty of New Echota in 1835.

Russell Thornton, a sociologist and a Cherokee, also challenges traditional views, on population losses resulting from removal. Thornton believes that a figure more than twice the traditional estimate of 4,000 would perhaps not be unreasonable. Using demographic projections and considering factors in addition to actual deaths, such as "desertions" and projected birth and death rates, Thornton suggests that more than 10,000 additional Cherokees would have lived during the period from 1835 to 1840 had it not been for forced removal.

Historian John R. Finger, who recently helped to establish the legal origin of the Eastern Band of Cherokees, examines the impact of the removal crises on those Cherokees who had a legal basis for remaining in North Carolina. He points out that Tsali, while not solely responsible for the Eastern Band, did have a profound influence on those who remained behind, symbolizing the Cherokee determination to remain in their ancestral home at all costs. Finger compares the resistance campaign of William Holland Thomas with the resistance campaign of Chief John Ross and de-

Introduction

scribes how the threat of removal ironically helped preserve and promote Cherokee tribalism.

Rennard Strickland, a lawyer of Cherokee descent, and his brother William discuss the effects of removal on the Cherokees who were forced west. They trace the 150-year period since the Trail of Tears, dividing it into six different time frames, in each of which the Cherokees met a unique set of challenges. The Cherokee Nation survives today, changed in many respects but in many others as near to the Cherokees of 1838 as the Cherokees of 1838 were to their ancestors 150 years earlier, the Cherokees of 1688.

The Cherokee removal of 1838 created havoc for the Cherokees, and some of the attendant problems—especially land loss and factionalism—still haunt them today. The insights and the information in the following six essays are varied and thought-provoking. Each should enlighten readers and encourage further study.

NOTES

1. Charles C. Royce, "The Cherokee Nation of Indians: A Narrative of their Official Relations with the Colonial and Federal Governments," Bureau of American Ethnology, *Fifth Annual Report, 1883–84* (Washington, D.C.: Government Printing Office, 1887), 256.

2. Bernard Sheehan, *Seeds of Extinction: Jeffersonian Philanthropy and the American Indian* (Chapel Hill: University of North Carolina Press, 1973), 119–47, 213–42.

3. Theda Perdue, *A Faithless Guardian: American Indian Policy, 1789–1840* (Arlington Heights, Ill.: Harlan Davidson, forthcoming). The civilization program was not the only means employed by the federal government to obtain Indian land. President John Adams's administration followed the example set by the British before the outbreak of the Revolution, that is, they sought to gain land cessions from the Cherokees by settling their overdue debts with trading companies or with the government-operated factory at Tellico in Cherokee country. This method of obtaining lands from the Indians continued through Thomas Jefferson's administration. In fact, the factory manager had instructions from Jefferson himself to keep the Cherokees in debt so that their lands could be more easily obtained by the government. Another method employed by Jefferson and his successors was to obtain Cherokee land through bribery. Sheehan, *Seeds of Extinction*, 171; Ronald N. Satz, *American Indian Policy in the Jacksonian Era* (Lincoln: University of Nebraska Press, 1975), 110–11.

4. For the best work on this period, see William G. McLoughlin, *Cherokee Renascence in the New Republic* (Princeton: Princeton University Press, 1986).

5. Sheehan, *Seeds of Extinction*, 119–47, 213–42.

6. For the specific terms of the 1817 treaty, see Royce, "Cherokee Nation of Indians," 84–85.

7. Grant Foreman, *Indians and Pioneers: The Story of the American Southwest Before 1830* (Norman: University of Oklahoma Press, 1930), 26, and McLoughlin, *Cherokee Renascence*, 128–45.

8. John R. Finger, *The Eastern Band of Cherokees, 1819–1900* (Knoxville: University of Tennessee Press, 1984), 10–11.

9. McLoughlin, *Cherokee Renascence*, 201–5.

10. Ibid., 367–68.

11. Mary Young, "The Cherokee Nation: Mirror of the Republic," *American Quarterly* 33 (Winter 1981): 501–25.

12. Reginald Horsman, *Race and Manifest Destiny: The Origin of American Racial Anglo-Saxonism* (Cambridge: Harvard University Press, 1981).

13. Although Adams set aside the treaty, a subsequent treaty in 1826 achieved the same cession. Michael D. Green, *The Politics of Indian Removal: Creek Government and Society in Crisis* (Lincoln: University of Nebraska Press, 1982), 98–125.

14. Charles Warren, *The Supreme Court in United States History*, 2 vols. (Boston: Little, Brown, 1926), 1:759–64; Satz, *American Indian Policy*, 49–52.

15. Francis Paul Prucha, *The Great Father: The United States Government and the American Indians*, 2 vols. (Lincoln: University of Nebraska Press, 1984), 1:213.

CHEROKEE REMOVAL
Before and After

Cherokee Land Use in Georgia Before Removal

DOUGLAS C. WILMS

The Cherokees living in Georgia prior to removal in 1838 were probably the most thoroughly acculturated Indians in nineteenth-century America. They were one of the first Indian groups to successfully transform their aboriginal landscape into a new cultural landscape that resembled and perhaps sometimes surpassed their white frontier neighbors. This essay reconstructs the new Cherokee cultural landscape as it appeared on the eve of their expulsion.[1] Such a reconstruction requires an examination of the early acculturative processes that prompted the Cherokees to adopt new settlement patterns, new approaches to land utilization, and new culture traits. These new developments reflected especially the influence of three groups: resident traders, missionaries, and government agents, each of whom made its own unique contribution to the acculturation process.

THE FUR TRADER AS AN AGENT OF CHANGE

Several significant changes in Cherokee land utilization began to occur when sustained contacts were begun with whites. Generally speaking, fur traders were the first Europeans to penetrate the wilderness in the seventeenth century and to act as agents of land use and cultural change. One of the first changes to take place resulted from the trader's role as a supplier

I

of manufactured goods. European manufactures contributed substantially to alteration of the traditional subsistence economy of the Cherokees. In exchange for peltries, the Indians sought firearms, hatchets, knives, traps, and other goods that increased their hunting efficiency.[2] These items not only permitted native Americans to raise their standard of living and to support themselves with less effort by gathering more furs and hides, but also led to a more rapid depletion of an area's game supply. As a result, these areas tended to be hunted less often by the Indians. As early as 1767, during negotiations between North Carolina and the Cherokee, one member of the tribe remarked, "True it is the deer, buffalo and the turkeys are almost gone . . . the white people eat hogs, cattle and other things which they have here, but our food is farther off."[3] This sequence of events became a recurring and predictable theme as the Cherokees withdrew toward the interior in the face of the advancing frontier settlements.

The second role of the trader as an agent of change was related to his own subsistence methods. Although he was primarily interested in gathering furs and skins, the trader also served as an acculturative agent in agricultural methods. James Mooney asserted that after the development of a regular trade some traders took Indian wives and established permanent residence in the Cherokee country. In Mooney's words, these individuals farmed and raised domestic livestock "according to civilized methods, thus even without intention, constituting themselves industrial teachers for the tribe."[4]

Eighteenth-century observers noted how quickly many Cherokees began to raise European crops and livestock. William Bartram carefully recorded his observations as he traveled through the Cherokee country in the 1770s. He wrote of meeting a trader who kept cattle and whose Cherokee wife made butter and cheese.[5] Bartram observed that in addition to game the Cherokee also ate "domestic poultry; and also of domestic kine, as beeves, goats, and swine—never horses' flesh, though they have horses in great plenty."[6]

European plants, animals, and agricultural techniques introduced by traders appear to have been gradually diffused throughout the nation; by the revolutionary period many Cherokees had become acquainted with most phases of European agriculture. Although traders do not appear to have intentionally introduced white agricultural and land-use practices, it is probable that some Cherokees saw the advantages of such a system as practiced by the trader and his family. No doubt a diminished game supply also encouraged acceptance of domesticated meat and vegetables.

Finally, traders may be viewed as agents of change because miscegenation was commonplace among them. The Cherokee intermarried with whites more than any other southeastern tribe did.[7] The mixed-blood offspring of these marriages dominated tribal government and played a crucial role during the nineteenth century. The mixed-blood group appears to have been more amenable to adopting white agricultural practices than the full bloods, who tended to be conservative, frequently clinging tenaciously to the old ways.

The role of the trader as an agent of change was at its peak in the eighteenth century—the initial period of acculturation and land-use change. Most trader-induced acculturation in the eighteenth century appears to have been accidental and unplanned, in sharp contrast with the concerted civilizing efforts of government agents and missionaries in the nineteenth century.

THE FEDERAL GOVERNMENT AS AN AGENT OF CHANGE

It has been suggested that the Cherokee embarked on a path of conscious acculturation shortly after the revolutionary war.[8] In addition to reflecting the efforts made by individual Cherokee, increasing acculturation at this time was also the result of the intentional efforts of the federal government and of missionary societies. These two agencies, often working together, deliberately fostered many of the "civilizing" processes that were to contribute to subsequent changes in Cherokee land use. By consciously fostering these processes they were unlike the traders, who brought about such changes in unplanned or accidental ways.

Although the policies of the United States government changed from time to time, its earliest efforts appear to have been sincere attempts to bring peace and "civilization" to the Cherokee. Government officials thought the "civilizing" process could be attained best by encouraging formal education and by introducing the white approach to agriculture

3

and industry. To accomplish these goals, the government made gifts of livestock and tools to the Indians, gave financial assistance to missionary societies, and appointed Indian agents to live among the tribe.

Agrarian reform was encouraged in 1793 when Congress began to appropriate funds annually for the purchase of livestock and implements for the Indians. The government rationalized that such gifts would help create a desire for private property and, in turn, would bring about a basic change in the Indian economy. Naturally, it was also hoped such changes would result in the Indians being content with less land.[9]

Two Moravians, Abraham Steiner and Frederick De Schweinitz, journeyed through the Cherokee country in 1799 seeking to establish a mission station. They wrote that the Cherokee "had greatly increased in culture and civilization in the last few years; that in the course of the last summer 300 plows and as many pairs of cotton carding-combs had been sent to this nation and they had begun to devote themselves to agriculture and the raising of cotton; had several times brought cotton for sale and they had themselves begun to spin and weave."[10] In addition to seeing cotton, corn, and wheat fields, the two Moravians observed that the inhabitants of the area were well supplied with all forms of livestock and poultry. Cherokees sold some produce to the local garrison, and droves of hogs were bought from and driven out of the Cherokee nation.[11]

Government policies toward the Cherokee encouraged and accelerated the new approaches to land use initiated by early fur traders. The federal government gave livestock and implements to the natives and appointed agents to demonstrate their use. In addition, financial assistance was given to missionary societies for establishing schools in the nation. Here, formal and vocational education, they hoped, would encourage civilization and help bring about other desirable changes in the Cherokee society and economy.

MISSIONARIES AS AGENTS OF CHANGE

As early as 1789, Secretary of War Henry Knox recommended that missionaries, supplied with the implements and livestock necessary for successful farming, be sent to live among the Indians.[12] His recommendation was adopted in 1819 when Congress created the Civilization Fund, an annual sum of $10,000 that was used to support Indian education. Because administrative procedures for distributing these modest funds did not exist, the government invited church and missionary societies to apply for the money for the schools they operated.[13] The money was regularly spent on items that could not be produced locally, for example, tools, plows, books, and writing paper.

For many years the Moravians had planned to establish a mission among the southern Indians. It was not until 1801, however, that their dreams were fulfilled. The mission, named Springplace, remained in operation until 1833. The missionary station itself served as an example to the Indians of European approach to land use—one that stressed plow cultivation and the raising of livestock.

An even more influential Cherokee mission was established in 1817 at Brainerd, near present-day Chattanooga, by the American Board of Commissioners for Foreign Missions. In conjunction with its mission schools in Indian territory, the board also established a school in Cornwall, Connecticut, where promising Indian students were sent for further instruction. The Brainerd mission worked closely with the federal government and had the distinction of being the first Indian mission in North America "to give instruction in systematic and scientific agriculture, also trade, domestic science, and domestic arts."[14] The emphasis on vocational training at Brainerd coincided with the prevailing educational philosophy of the federal government. By 1820 the Brainerd mission was a model agricultural station, whose resident farmers, blacksmiths, and mechanics served as examples to the Cherokee of the new male role. These men also played an important educational role as they demonstrated cropping procedures, care of livestock, and the building and maintenance of gristmills and dams.[15]

The influence of the missionary as an agent of change in the Cherokee nation must be viewed in terms of his dual efforts to formally educate the young and to encourage systematic and intensive agriculture. The mission stations served as model farms occupied by white men who were not interested in acquiring Cherokee land. The missionaries lived in close contact with the Cherokee for long periods of time. Their interest in improving the lot of the Cherokee was self-evident, for they deliberately—and by example—educated their wards in the fundamentals of writing, agriculture, and industry.

AGRARIAN PROGRESS IN THE NINETEENTH CENTURY

Article fourteen of the 1791 Treaty of Holston officially encouraged the Cherokee to become farmers. Progress along these lines was verified eighteen years later when a systematic census of the Cherokee was taken under the auspices of the Cherokee Indian agent Return Jonathan Meigs.[16] His report of the 1809 census revealed that there were 12,395 Cherokees, 583 Negro slaves, and 314 whites living in the nation. The census stated that the improvements and property acquired "has principally been done since 1796." Thus it would seem that within little more than a decade many Cherokee had acquired the skills, tools, and livestock necessary to establish the foundation of an agrarian economy.

Much of this progress was reconfirmed in 1824 when the Cherokee themselves took a census of their nation.[17] Information from this census is listed with similar material from the earlier one taken by Meigs in 1809 (see table 1). If these data are assumed to be essentially correct, a significant number of changes had taken place during the fifteen years between censuses. The native population grew by 30 percent and the number of slaves reached 1,277, an increase of 119 percent. A greater number of children were attending private and mission schools. Some Cherokee men owned and operated gristmills and sawmills; spinning wheels appear to have been found in virtually every Cherokee home. On the farms, the number of plows had increased by 416 percent, and domesticated horses, cattle, swine, sheep, and goats totaled nearly 80,000. Stores, blacksmith shops, and even a threshing machine were in operation. The character of the material goods possessed by the Cherokee clearly suggests that, by the mid-1820s, they were becoming a nation of Anglo-style farmers.

The noted missionary Samuel Worcester wrote in 1830 that agriculture was the principal employment and support of the Cherokee people. He suggested that hunting as a way of life had been completely abandoned. With regard to those who lived by the chase he commented, "I certainly have not found them, not even heard of them, except from the floor of Congress, and other distant sources of information."[18]

In December 1830, a group of resident missionaries met at New Echota and issued a statement that included a thorough report on agricultural progress. It noted that "thirty years ago a plough was scarcely seen in the nation. Twenty years ago there were nearly 500. Still the ground was cul-

Cherokee Land Use in Georgia

TABLE 1
Cherokee Nation Intercensus Changes, 1809–24

	Meigs Census of 1809	Cherokee Nation Census of 1824	% of Change 1809–24
Population[a]	12,395	16,060	30
Negro slaves	583	1,277	119
Whites	314	215	−29
Schools	5	18	260
Students	94	314	234
Gristmills	13	36	177
Sawmills	3	13	333
Looms	429	762	78
Spinning wheels	1,572	2,486	58
Wagons	30	172	473
Plows	567	2,923	416
Horses	6,519	7,683	18
Black cattle	19,165	22,531	18
Swine	19,778	46,732	136
Sheep	1,037	2,566	147
Goats	—	430	—
Blacksmith shops	—	62	—
Stores	—	9	—
Tanyards	—	2	—
Powder mills	1	1	—
Threshing machines	—	1	—

Sources: Cherokee Census of 1809, Moravian Archives, Winston-Salem, N.C.; Cherokee Census of 1824, in Laws of the Cherokee Nation (Knoxville, Tenn.: Heiskell and Brown, 1826).

[a] These figures include only Cherokees.

tivated chiefly by the hoe only. Six years ago the number of ploughs, as enumerated, was 2,923. Among us all, we scarcely know a field which is now cultivated without ploughing."[19]

Trade and commerce were facilitated by the numerous roads that traversed the nation. Figure 1 depicts the roads as they existed in about 1825. Most of these were built by the United States under the treaty of 1816, which also gave the federal government the right to free navigation of all rivers within the Cherokee nation.[20] Several Cherokee established taverns along these roads and profited from the traffic.

Cherokee trade was generally restricted to the sale of corn, livestock, and

7

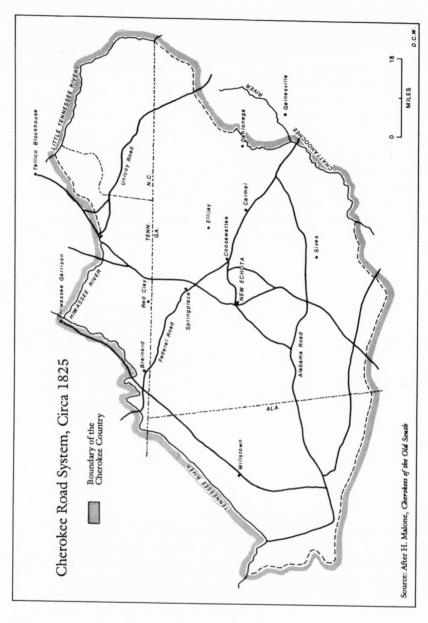

Cherokee Road System, Circa 1825

Boundary of the
Cherokee Country

Source: After H. Malone, *Cherokees of the Old South*

Figure I.

domestic hides; most trade was overland with adjacent states. Dr. Elizur Butler, a missionary at Haweis, wrote that many Cherokee, including full bloods, raised meat and corn for sale. "Last season, while traveling on the frontiers of Georgia, I well recollect seeing wagon loads of corn going from the nation to the different states. Droves of cattle and hogs are driven annually from the nation to the different states. A few weeks since, not less than 200 beeves were driven from this vicinity to the northern market; and I think as great numbers were collected in previous years."[21]

By the mid 1830s the Cherokee had become a nation of Anglo-style farmers and had progressed far toward developing an agrarian economy. Although industry was less developed, trade in agricultural commodities flourished as grain and livestock surpluses mounted. The Cherokee, more than any other tribe, made great strides toward adopting white agricultural techniques, and their cultural landscape was beginning to reflect the changes.

THE 1832 LAND LOTTERY

In 1831 Georgia's surveyors entered the Cherokee territory pursuant to a legislative act passed the previous year. Cherokee Georgia covered more than 6,000 square miles, and the Georgia surveyors divided it into four sections, the dividing lines of each running north to south (figure 2). Each section was, in turn, divided into a number of districts, each of which was 9 square miles. The districts, in turn, were divided into either 160-acre land lots or 40-acre gold lots (figure 2) that were to be distributed among Georgia citizens in the upcoming lottery.[22]

Finally, the surveyors delivered to the surveyor general plats representative of each lot. These plats were two inches square and depicted the streams, quality of land, and extent of Indian improvements found on each lot.[23] A sample plat, representing lot 37 in the sixth district of the first section, shows Nuntoolly Creek surrounded by oak and hickory land (figure 3). Along the southern boundary is a three-acre Indian improvement.[24] The materials compiled by Georgia's surveyors constitute the most accurate early source available for studying Cherokee settlement patterns.

The morphology of Cherokee towns apparently differed from that of towns in other areas of frontier America. Instead of compact settlements

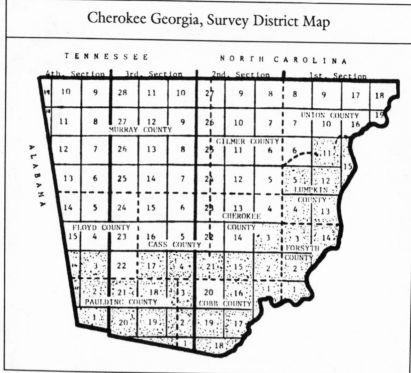

Figure 2. The stippled area represents the Gold Districts. Broken lines show the boundaries of the ten counties created in 1832. Compiled by Marion Hemperley, Georgia Surveyor-General Department. Reproduced with permission.

with contiguous homesites, Cherokee towns consisted of loosely clustered homesteads whose dwellings were separated from each other by surrounding woodland. Benjamin F. Currey, an agent for Indian removal, noted that "under Cherokee laws, as they now stand and have stood for many years past, each family has a right to clear and cultivate as much land as he pleases, so long as he does not go nearer than a quarter mile to his neighbor, and has a right to object to and prevent his neighbor from improving or cultivating land within less than a quarter mile of his fence."[25]

Surrounding woodland was probably viewed by Cherokee as a resource

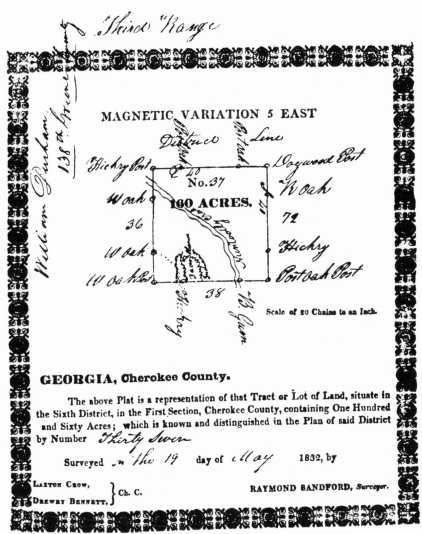

Figure 3. Example of a survey plat depicting an Indian improvement as housed in the official records of the Georgia Surveyor-General Department. Reproduced with permission.

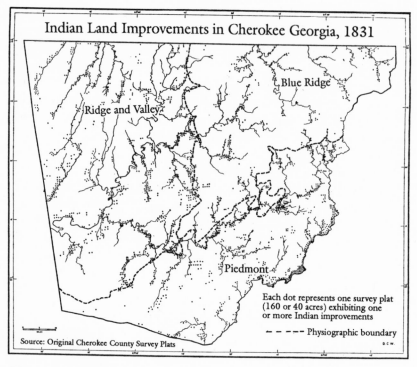

Indian Land Improvements in Cherokee Georgia, 1831

Blue Ridge

Ridge and Valley

Piedmont

Each dot represents one survey plat
(160 or 40 acres) exhibiting one
or more Indian improvements

‒ ‒ ‒ ‒ ‒ Physiographic boundary
D.C.W.

Source: Original Cherokee County Survey Plats

Figure 4.

that was integral and necessary to the normal functioning of a homestead.
Here hogs and cattle could forage and small game could be hunted and
trapped. Moreover, the woodland was a source of fuel, wild fruits, and
nuts, as well as building and fencing materials. Although these clusters of
scattered homesteads were often called towns, there is no evidence that
urban activities were of any significance. The dispersed and linear village
settlement pattern was a relatively new phenomenon among the Cherokee. Figure 4 was constructed to present the locational pattern of all the
improved lands identified from survey records. The largest concentrations
of improved land were situated in the fertile lowlands of the Ridge and
Valley province.

It has been suggested that early southeastern Indians practiced a riverine
agriculture and took advantage of alluvial soils that could easily be worked

with crude tools.[26] This suggestion was based in part on the recorded observations of early traders and travelers, who noted repeatedly that Indian fields were adjacent to the banks of streams. The locational patterns of improved tracts depicted in figure 5 support this contention and suggest that even after the Cherokees acquired the use of the plow, they still recognized the value of cultivating the alluvial lowlands. Cherokee preference for bottomlands probably reflected the superior fertility of soils in such localities and the ease with which they could be cultivated.

A sample area in the Ridge and Valley province was examined at a large scale in an attempt to locate improved lots precisely with respect to streams and floodplains. All improved lots in the sample area were plotted on a topographic map with a scale of one inch to one mile.[27] The sample area is in the vicinity of Calhoun, Georgia, where the Conasauga and Coosawattee rivers join to form the Oostanaula River. The locations of improved lots in relation to the floodplains are presented in figure 5. The Cherokee preference for floodplain sites is strikingly revealed.

THE CHEROKEE CENSUS OF 1835

In an attempt to identify and enumerate characteristics of Indian population, landholdings, and agriculture, United States government officials took a census of the Cherokee Nation in 1835, which was the most comprehensive and complete inventory of the Cherokees up to that time. The census of 1835 enumerated a total of 9,780 individuals in Cherokee Georgia, which, if correct, indicates a population density of 1.4 persons per square mile. Of the total population, 8,936 were Cherokees, 776 were slaves, and 68 were intermarried whites.[28] There were 1,357 families counted in the census, and the average size of a Cherokee family was 6.6 persons.

Figure 6 depicts Cherokee Georgia's population distribution as of 1835. The majority of the Cherokee lived in the alluvial lowlands in the western part of the study area, while relatively few lived in the areas that bordered Georgia on the east and south. The small population in these areas probably reflected two conditions. First, the Blue Ridge Mountains area was less attractive to the majority of Cherokee, who had become sedentary farmers and who probably preferred the more attractive river bottoms of larger streams in the Piedmont and Ridge and Valley provinces. A greater

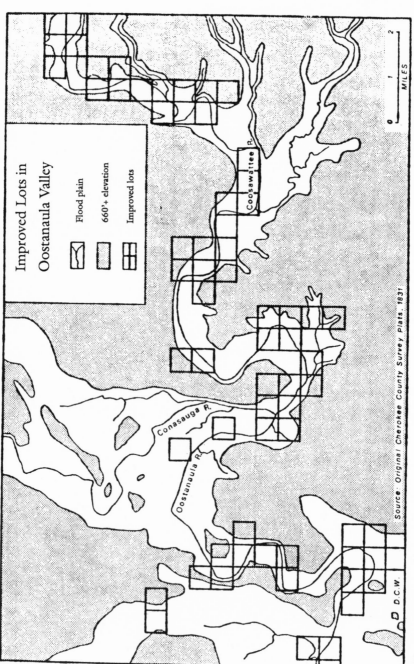

**Improved Lots in
Oostanaula Valley**

Flood plain

660'+ elevation

Improved lots

Coosawattee R.

Conasauga R.

Oostanaula R.

Source: Original Cherokee County Survey Plats. 1831

D.C.W.

0 1 2
MILES

Figure 5.

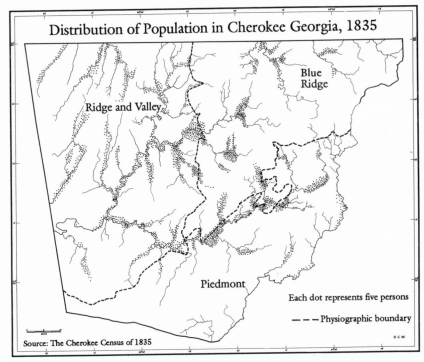

Figure 6.

extent of available bottomlands would have meant that more families and kin could locate within close proximity to each other. Second, and perhaps more important, the peripheral area of eastern Cherokee Georgia had witnessed increasing incursions of many lawless white prospectors since the discovery of gold near Auroria in July 1829.[29]

Large population concentrations occurred along physiographic boundaries, especially at those points where streams flowed from one province to another and where streams closely paralleled a boundary. The greatest concentrations were found along the Piedmont–Blue Ridge and Ridge and Valley–Blue Ridge boundaries. These locations were undoubtedly viewed as favorable sites because they gave residents access to differing resources within each physiographic province, particularly the better farmland in the Piedmont and Ridge and Valley areas and a variety of wood, fruits, nuts, fish, and game in the Blue Ridge.

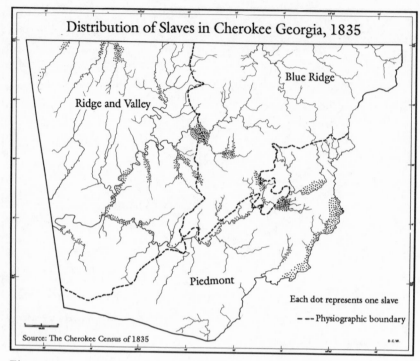

Figure 7.

Figure 7 depicts the distribution of slave residents in Cherokee Georgia. Slaves were concentrated along the larger streams of the Piedmont and Ridge and Valley provinces, while relatively few lived in the Blue Ridge area. In the Piedmont, most slaves were concentrated in two river valleys, the Etowah and Chattahoochee. In the Ridge and Valley area slaves were more widely dispersed along the banks of a number of large streams. Most slaves resided in counties that also had a sizable mixed-blood population. Of the 1,357 families in Cherokee Georgia, only 96, or 7 percent, owned slaves. Mixed-blood families, including those with an intermarried white resident, owned the overwhelming majority. Only 13 full-blood families in Cherokee Georgia owned any slaves.

The Cherokee census of 1835 lists 1,737 farms, which accounted for a total of 19,351 cultivated acres.[30] There were 1,980 farmers in the area who were eighteen years of age and over. This figure exceeds the total number of families and gives an average of 1.5 farmers per family, an indication of the importance of farming among the Cherokees. An average of 11.1 acres of land was cultivated for each farm in Cherokee Georgia.[31] Corn was the most important crop raised by the Cherokee. Production figures indicate that a total of 269,000 bushels were raised during the year of the census. Residents of Cherokee Georgia overall appear to have sold 25 percent of all corn raised, but some residents sold even larger percentages.

ROADS AND COMMERCE

Any discussion of surplus agricultural products should be accompanied by an examination of available transportation routes. The important Brainerd, Alabama, and Federal roads crossed the area and connected it with neighboring states. In addition, a number of other roads in this area converged upon the Cherokee capital of New Echota. These roads not only allowed the Cherokee to ship surplus agricultural products out of the area, but also permitted travelers and drovers to cross Cherokee Georgia on their way to neighboring states. Surplus corn and livestock raised by the Cherokee usually were sold in neighboring Tennessee, Georgia, and South Carolina.[32]

Thousands of hogs, cattle, horses, and mules were annually driven from Tennessee and Kentucky to eastern markets in the early 1800s. There was also an internal demand for livestock in the Southeast. In 1836, 40,000 hogs were driven to food-deficit cotton-producing areas in middle Alabama and Georgia.[33] Many drovers from Tennessee and Kentucky passed through the Cherokee Nation on their way to Georgia, and their herds consumed vast amounts of corn at various public houses or "stock stands" along the way. A drove of hogs may have varied from several hundred to several thousand head and could travel an estimated eight to twelve miles each day, and perhaps more, depending on the size of the herd. On the average, approximately twenty-four bushels of corn were consumed daily per thousand hogs.[34]

FIGURE 8
Appraisal of Property of Rising Fawn

Dwelling House 16 × 16 with shed and Puncheon floor	$30.00
Kitchen	10.00
Stable	3.00
Field 15 acres @ $6.00 per acre	90.00
Field 3 acres @ $6.00 per acre	18.00
8 apple trees @ $3.00	12.00
8 small trees (fruit) @ $1.00	8.00
20 Peach trees @ $0.50	10.00
	$205.00

Source: Appraisal of Rising Fawn, September 12, 1836, 2, in *Valuations of Cherokee Property in Floyd and Walker, Georgia, No. 23,* by Hemphill and Liddell, Bureau of Indian Affairs, Record Group 75, National Archives, Washington, D.C.

PROPERTY EVALUATIONS

The Treaty of New Echota was concluded on December 29, 1835, and was ratified on May 23, 1836. Government agents began to canvass the Cherokee country to fulfill the requirements for a "just and fair valuation" of all Cherokee improvements. It was the task of the appraising or valuing agents, as they were called, to assign cash values to all improvements made by each Cherokee on his homestead. The agents, working in pairs, kept detailed records and noted the name of each homestead owner, the location of his homestead, and the number, type, and value of all his improvements.[35] The evaluation of Cherokee improvements was made during the years 1836–37 and thus complements the information provided by the Cherokee census of 1835. See figure 8 for a sample appraisal.

The valuations of 1836–37 showed a total of 35,285 acres in cultivated fields, the majority of which were found along streams in the Ridge and Valley area (figure 9). Nearly 80,000 fruit trees were enumerated by the appraising agents.[36] With 63,000 trees, the peach was the most numerous and commonplace variety and was found on nearly every Cherokee homestead (figure 10). Apples were the second most popular fruit, while cherry, pear, quince, and plum trees were of minor significance.

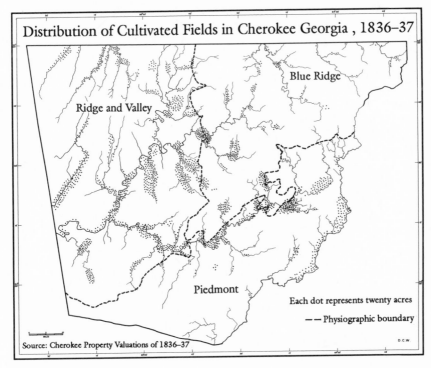

Distribution of Cultivated Fields in Cherokee Georgia , 1836–37

Blue Ridge

Ridge and Valley

Piedmont

Each dot represents twenty acres

— — Physiographic boundary

Source: Cherokee Property Valuations of 1836–37

D.C.W.

Figure 9.

Peaches were an important crop in early American agriculture. They were grown in Virginia as early as 1633 and were cultivated in Georgia shortly after the colony was founded.[37] John Lawson, the surveyor-general of North Carolina, reported that Indians gave him dried and stewed peaches as he traveled through that state in the early eighteenth century.[38] The Cherokee Indians in nineteenth-century Georgia undoubtedly used their peaches in the same manner as neighboring whites. First, peaches were either sun, air, or kiln-dried and were consumed during the autumn and winter months.[39] Second, it was a common practice to feed peaches to hogs. This fruit was so plentiful in many areas that hogs were allowed to scavenge among the trees and orchards for the fruit and kernels that had dropped to the ground.[40] It is also possible that a diet including dried peaches was fed to hogs each evening to induce them to return to a home-

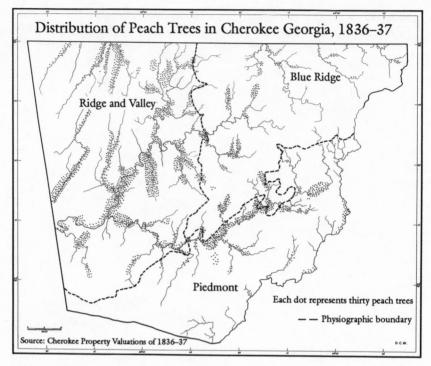

Figure 10.

stead after a day of mast feeding in nearby woods. Finally, peaches were used for making brandy.[41]

The Cherokee census of 1835 showed that the majority of Cherokee Georgia's population lived in the Ridge and Valley area, and the valuations of 1836–37 indicated that the majority of dwellings and outbuildings were also there (figure 11). Most of the corn and wheat was raised in this area, and the largest corn surplus and most of the corncribs were found there (figure 12). Mills and ferries were more widespread throughout Cherokee Georgia, with the majority of mills found in the peripheral area and most ferries found in the Ridge and Valley region. In terms of acres cultivated, number of fruit trees, and total value of all improvements, the Ridge and Valley region was again the dominant area. With the exception of mills and ferries, this area had a majority in every category itemized in the valuations and

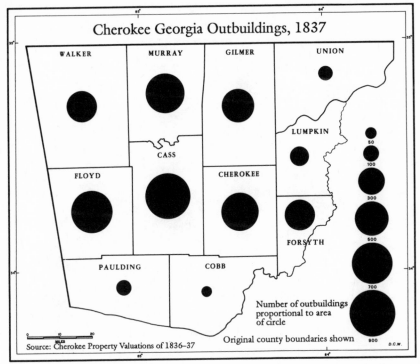

Figure II.

exceeded the combined figures for the Blue Ridge and peripheral areas. Perhaps the most striking category was property values. Property in the Ridge and Valley area was appraised at $543,801.26, a figure representing 70 percent of the value of all improvements in Cherokee Georgia.

The data derived from the property valuations support and amplify the findings gleaned from the 1835 census. The numerous dwellings, outbuildings, fruit trees, and cultivated fields clearly indicate that the Cherokee had by the time of their removal become a sedentary agrarian group who had rapidly adopted a new approach to land use. Extremes in standards of living existed, however, as seen by the number of improvements made by some and not by others. While many Cherokee lived in small cabins and cultivated few acres, others had many improvements and lived among more comfortable surroundings. More than a few were wealthy. The most sig-

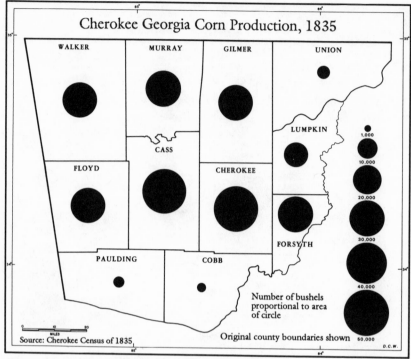

Figure 12.

nificant point, perhaps, is that the Cherokees had become an acculturated group who had exchanged their traditional approach to land utilization for one that was similar to that of their white neighbors.

Throughout Cherokee Georgia larger than average homesteads tended to be located where roads crossed principal streams or where two important roads intersected. In many cases, area residents also owned and operated stores, ferries, and mills at these strategic points. The large amounts of surplus corn available, the number of slave residents, the numerous corncribs, and the many livestock pens in these areas support the assumption that farms located there had commercial orientations. Residents of such areas undoubtedly produced surplus agricultural commodities to sell both to travelers passing through Cherokee Georgia and to residents of neighboring states. Moreover, Cherokee merchants probably made livestock and grain purchases from local Cherokee farmers from time to time.

The geographical analysis leading to this period reconstruction adds a new dimension to what has been known of the historical Cherokees prior to removal from their homes in the East. This dimension, focusing upon human occupancy patterns, not only has substantiated Cherokee progress in various fields of endeavor, but also has identified and attempted to explain why areas of intense demographic and economic activity existed where they did.

The process of acculturation had produced new land-use patterns in Cherokee Georgia by the 1830s, which are revealed by an analysis of the Cherokee census of 1835 and the property valuations of 1836–37. Hunting was obviously no longer of paramount importance as more and more Cherokees cleared land, established farms, made improvements, fenced their fields, and raised domesticated crops and livestock. Plows were in use throughout the nation, stores and blacksmith shops dotted the countryside, and gristmills and sawmills were in operation. One of the most impressive changes occurred in the number of livestock that the Cherokee had acquired by the second decade of the nineteenth century. With nearly 80,000 head, the Cherokees clearly were no longer dependent upon game animals. Perhaps the most significant aspect of the cultural landscape was the impressive number of permanent structures that characterized Cherokee Georgia. More than 6,000 privately owned dwellings and outbuildings mirror the significance of agrarian operations for these people in the late 1830s. In addition to the numerous and widespread corncribs, cabins, kitchens, and smokehouses, an assortment of other structures such as fences, livestock pens, and fish traps reflect the Cherokees' total commitment to agriculture as an accepted way of life.

The average Cherokee family lived in a modest log cabin on their own farmstead, where they cultivated about eleven acres. Corn was the main crop, and the average yield for Cherokee Georgia was 13.8 bushels per acre. They also raised a variety of vegetables, tended a large number of fruit trees, and probably raised some cotton for their own use as well. Hogs and cattle were the main source of meat, and occasionally surpluses of grain and livestock were sold in neighboring states and to travelers and drovers who passed through Cherokee Georgia. In addition to a dwelling, the average Cherokee owned one or two outbuildings. The ubiquitous corncrib was the most commonplace of all outbuildings in Cherokee Georgia, and many inhabitants owned at least one.

It is unfortunate that the land-use patterns of the average Cherokee farmer were not more widely known throughout the United States in the 1830s. Had this been the case, the Cherokee might have found more allies in Congress when the controversial removal bill was being debated. As it was, only a handful of missionaries and government agents could vouch for their achievements. The Cherokee themselves were aware of their accomplishments, and this knowledge probably accounted for part of their staunch resistance to removal. Having worked hard in clearing land and building improvements—precisely those endeavors missionaries and government agents had encouraged—most Cherokee refused to leave their farms.

Cherokee who resisted acculturation and were unwilling to change their forms of livelihood began migrating to areas west of the Mississippi River earlier, in the latter part of the eighteenth century. There they practiced their hunting-farming economy, unmolested for a while at least by the intrusion of white settlers. Left behind were tribal members who were unwilling to abandon their lands but were agreeable to applying new, more intensive uses to them. This group of Cherokee, probably the most thoroughly acculturated Indians in nineteenth-century America, adopted new culture traits and new patterns of settlement and land use. They were one of the first Indian groups to successfully transform their aboriginal landscape into a new cultural landscape—one with many farms, houses, outbuildings, ferries, and roads. These structures, which were finally abandoned in 1838, were evidence that the Cherokee had come a long way in their attempts to achieve a life-style similar to that of other frontier Americans.

NOTES

1. Data for the reconstruction were obtained from three principal sources. Two of these are the Cherokee Census of 1835 (also known as the Henderson Roll,

1835) and the Cherokee Property Valuations of 1836–37, both in Cherokee Removal Records, Record Group 75, National Archives, Washington, D.C. See Edward E. Hill, comp., *Preliminary Inventory of the Records of the Bureau of Indian Affairs*, vol. 1 (Record Group 75), National Archives Publication no. 65-9 (Washington, D.C., 1965), 75–76. These documents consist of appraisals of the value of Cherokee lands, improvements, and other property and assets. The appraisals were made by federal enumerators prior to Cherokee removal to areas west of the Mississippi River. The enumerators were obliged to visit each Cherokee family and to itemize and appraise all stationary improvements for later compensation. Their records were of immense value in locating and assessing Cherokee land-use patterns.

The third principal source, which was used for reconstructing early settlement patterns, is the collection of plats, maps, and field notebooks prepared by surveyors in preparation for the state of Georgia's 1832 land lottery. These records are housed in Surveyor-General Department of the Office of the Secretary of State, Archives and Records Building, Atlanta, Ga. In 1831 Georgia sent nearly one hundred surveyors into Cherokee Georgia to systematically divide the area into 160-acre land lots and 40-acre gold lots (figure 2). These lots were to be distributed among Georgia citizens in a lottery that was to be held the following year. Each surveyor was required to submit to the Georgia surveyor-general a plat of each lot. On these plats the surveyors recorded the streams, land features, and location of improvements made by Indians. In most cases the sizes of the Indian improvements were also noted. Field notebooks, district maps, and more than 55,000 plats were examined to determine the sizes and locations of all Cherokee improvements recorded by the surveyors. Locating improvements by lots permitted accurate mapping and revealed the overall settlement patterns of nineteenth-century Cherokee Georgia.

2. Guns were traded to the Cherokee in the early 1700s. See James Mooney, "Myths of the Cherokees," Bureau of American Ethnology, *Nineteenth Annual Report, 1897–98*, pt. 1 (Washington, D.C.: Government Printing Office, 1900), 213.

3. Louis De Vorsey, *The Indian Boundary in the Southern Colonies, 1763–1775* (Chapel Hill: University of North Carolina Press, 1966), 102.

4. Mooney, "Myths of the Cherokees," 213.

5. *The Travels of William Bartram: Naturalist's Edition*, ed. Francis Harper (New Haven: Yale University Press, 1958), 221.

6. William Bartram, "The Creek and Cherokee Indians," *Transactions of the American Ethnological Society*, vol. 3, pt. 1 (New York: George F. Putnam, 1852), 47.

7. Grant Foreman, *The Five Civilized Tribes* (Norman: University of Oklahoma Press, 1934), 360.

8. Raymond D. Fogelson and Paul Kutsche, "Cherokee Economic Coopera-

tives: The Gadugi," in *Symposium on Cherokee and Iroquois Culture,* ed. William N. Fenton and John Bulick, Smithsonian Institution, Bureau of American Ethnology Bulletin no. 180 (Washington, D.C.: Government Printing Office, 1961), 98. For an interesting viewpoint on this conscious acculturation, see William G. McLoughlin, "Who Civilized the Cherokees?" *Journal of Cherokee Studies* 13 (1988): 55–81.

9. William T. Hagan, *American Indians* (Chicago: University of Chicago Press, 1961), 45.

10. Samuel Cole Williams, *Early Travels in the Tennessee Country, 1540–1800* (Johnson City, Tenn.: Watauga Press, 1928), 459. For the complete story of the missionaries and the Cherokees, see William G. McLoughlin, *Cherokees and Missionaries, 1789–1839* (New Haven: Yale University Press, 1984).

11. Ibid., 464–90.

12. *American State Papers: Indian Affairs,* 1:54.

13. Hagan, *American Indians,* 87–88.

14. Robert S. Walker, *Torchlight to the Cherokees: The Brainerd Mission* (New York: Macmillan, 1931), 146.

15. Ibid., 142–43.

16. Photostatic copy of original in Moravian Archives, Winston-Salem, N.C.

17. *Laws of the Cherokee Nation* (Knoxville, Tenn.: Heiskell and Brown, 1826).

18. Jack Frederick Kilpatrick and Anna Gritts Kilpatrick, eds., *New Echota Letters* (Dallas: Southern Methodist University Press, 1969), 79.

19. Ibid., 86.

20. Charles C. Royce, "The Cherokee Nation of Indians: A Narrative of their Official Relations with the Colonial and Federal Governments," Bureau of American Ethnology, *Fifth Annual Report, 1883–84* (Washington, D.C.: Government Printing Office, 1887), 198.

21. *Cherokee Phoenix,* September 22, 1830.

22. Douglas C. Wilms, "Georgia's Land Lottery of 1832," *Chronicles of Oklahoma* 52 (Spring 1974): 52–60.

23. *Acts of the General Assembly of the State of Georgia, 1830* (Milledgeville, Ga.: Camak and Ragland, 1831), 128–31.

24. The field notebooks, district maps, and plat books are stored in the Georgia Surveyor-General Department and constitute the principal sources of information for this section.

25. *Correspondence on The subject of the Emigration of Indians,* 23d Cong., 1st sess., S. Doc. 512, 4:195.

26. Christopher Murphy and Charles Hudson, "On the Problem of Intensive Agriculture in the Aboriginal Southeastern United States," University of Geor-

gia, Department of Sociology and Anthropology, *Working Papers in Sociology and Anthropology 2* (April 1968): 27.

27. *Calhoun Georgia Quadrangle,* scale 1:62,500 (Washington, D.C.: U.S. Geological Survey, 1949).

28. The Cherokee Nation as a whole included 16,632 Cherokee, 1,592 slaves, and 201 white residents.

29. E. Merton Coulter, *Georgia: A Short History* (Chapel Hill: University of North Carolina Press, 1947), 233.

30. Census enumerators listed 614,400 tillable acres for Cherokee Georgia and valued them at $2 per acre for a total of $1,228,800. The amount of land cultivated by Indians was listed as 19,216 acres; however, the author's computations show that 19,351 acres is the correct figure.

31. Cultivated land is understood to be land that was tillable, for example, prepared, loosened, or plowed. Orchards and wooded land used for mast grazing would have been parts of a functional farmstead but would not have been considered cultivated land.

32. The driving of hogs to Georgia must have been a profitable venture as early as 1807. At that time the Moravian missionaries at Springplace attempted to buy hogs from their wealthy neighbor Joseph Vann, but he refused to sell any because he was preparing to take a large herd to Georgia. See Bishop Kenneth G. Hamilton, "Minutes of the Mission Conference Held in Springplace," *Atlanta Historical Bulletin* (Winter 1970): 46.

33. Lewis C. Gray, *History of Agriculture in the Southern United States to 1860,* 2 vols., Carnegie Institute of Washington Publication no. 430 (reprint, New York: Peter Smith, 1941), 1:837–40. An excellent study of pork production in the southern states is found in Sam B. Hilliard, "Pork in the Ante-Bellum South: The Geography of Self-sufficiency," *Annals of the Association of American Geographers* 59 (September 1969): 461–80.

34. Gray, *History of Agriculture* 1:841.

35. The term *improvement* referred to cleared and cultivated fields, dwellings, outbuildings, mills, ferries, gardens, lots, fruit trees, and such miscellaneous holdings as cut rails, boards, fences, ditches, wells, ponds, and fish traps.

36. The six varieties of fruit trees included peaches, apples, cherries, pears, plums, and quince.

37. H. P. Gould, *Peach-Growing* (New York: Macmillan, 1918), 5–7; James C. Bonner, *A History of Georgia Agriculture, 1732–1860* (Athens: University of Georgia Press, 1964), 150–51.

38. John Lawson, *Lawson's History of North Carolina* (London, 1714), 25–30.

39. Hamilton, "Minutes of the Mission Conference Held in Springplace," 33. The map that accompanies this article shows the Moravian mission at Springplace (p. 8). Apple and peach orchards are shown as well as a small structure with the notation "Kiln for drying peaches."

40. Gould, *Peach-Growing,* 8; Lyman Carrier, *The Beginnings of Agriculture in America* (New York: McGraw-Hill, 1923), 198.

41. Bonner, *History of Georgia Agriculture,* 150–51.

Rhetoric Versus Reality: The Indian Policy of Andrew Jackson

RONALD N. SATZ

Andrew Jackson is certainly one of the most fascinating of all American presidents. He was one of those rare individuals who left his imprint on an era. As one scholar has noted, "he was a man of such force, so invincibly controversial, so widely believed to be either avenging angel or devil, that his own personality alone explains in large part the historical appeal of the era that he seemed both to symbolize and dominate."[1] Although generations of historians have subjected the so-called Age of Jackson to close scrutiny, there is still a great deal of controversy about the man and his era. One of the more controversial topics is Jackson's Indian policy.[2]

In March 1837, when Jackson was preparing to leave the White House for retirement at the Hermitage in Nashville, Indian land occupancy east of the Mississippi River was but a fraction of what it had been eight years earlier. During his two terms in office, Jackson played a major role in the dispossession of eastern Indians from their tribal domains. War Department officials negotiated nearly seventy Indian treaties that were ratified by the Senate (a record unequaled by any other administration), and the overwhelming majority of them involved land cessions.[3]

Jackson had sought congressional approval of his removal policy very early during his first term by enthusiastically recommending and vigorously pushing the Indian Removal Act through both houses of Congress in 1830. This law empowered the president to negotiate treaties providing for the voluntary relocation of eastern Indians to the trans-Mississippi West.[4] By 1837, the Jackson administration had removed 46,000 Indians and had secured treaties providing for the removal of a slightly larger number. Jackson's Indian policy had opened about 100 million acres of land in the West. Only a few scattered remnants of the great tribes that had once dwelled east of the Mississippi River were without treaty stipulations requiring their relocation when the president said farewell to the nation's capital.[5]

The Indian removal policy was a controversial issue during the 1830s.[6] President Jackson assured congressional leaders and the American people that such a policy would enable the federal government to place the Indians in a region where they would be free of white encroachment and jurisdictional disputes between the federal and state governments. Indians wishing to remain in the East would receive land allotments and become citizens of the state in which they resided. Jackson claimed the policy would be "generous to the Indians" and, at the same time, would allow the United States to "exercise a parental control over their interests and possibly perpetuate their race."[7] However, while Jackson may have pursued his policy with the self-assurance that his motives and methods were beyond reproach, not all Americans were swayed by his rhetoric.

Opponents of Jackson's Indian removal policy constituted a large, diverse, and vocal group of Americans. Notable among these critics were the president's political adversaries. Indeed, the debate preceding the passage of the Removal Act sparked the first major partisan battle of Old Hickory's presidency.[8] Some of Jackson's opponents, like the politically astute Henry Clay of Kentucky, had previously argued that Indians were inferior to whites and that their disappearance from the face of the earth would be no great loss. Clay apparently changed his position when Indian removal became associated with Jackson in the public's mind.[9] Other critics of the Removal Act, such as Sen. Theodore Frelinghuysen of New Jersey, attacked the policy on deeply rooted moral grounds. Frelinghuysen, a fervent evangelical Protestant, envisioned his opposition as a way of promoting Christian benevolence.[10] Regardless of their motivation, the president's adversaries all shared at least one basic fear: they envisioned Jackson as a despot who was ready to force his will on the Indians even if that meant their destruction as a people.[11]

Generations of scholars have relied on and echoed the rhetoric found in the commentaries, speeches, and correspondence of the opponents of Indian removal when writing their accounts of Jackson's policies. These writers have presented what has been called a "devil theory" of Old Hickory's role in Indian affairs. Their accounts depict him as a ruthless Indian-hater intent upon dispossessing and, according to some, even annihilating the eastern tribes.[12] While many contemporary authors have erroneously argued or implied that emigration to the West was obligatory for all eastern Indians under the terms of the Removal Act itself, others have focused attention on Jackson's implementation of that legislation, and some have even equated his removal policy with Adolph Hitler's "final solution" to the so-called Jewish problem in Nazi Germany.[13]

Ronald T. Takaki, a historian of race and culture in America, refers to President Jackson as "the nation's confidence man," who developed "a metaphysics for genocide." According to Takaki, Jackson "recognized the need to explain the nation's conduct toward Indians, to give it moral meaning. In his writings, messages to Congress, and personal letters, Jackson presented a philosophical justification for the extermination of native Americans." Takaki, borrowing language from the English author and literary critic D. H. Lawrence, asks of Jackson, "What sort of a white man is he?" And, again using Lawrence's words, he replies, "Why, he is a man with a gun. He is a killer, a slayer. Patient and gentle as he is, he is a slayer. Self-effacing . . . still he is a killer."[14]

Among the more controversial studies written by advocates of the devil theory are those by scholars who have attempted to explain Jackson's actions through the use of psychohistory. They generally assume that Old Hickory hated Indians and proceed to offer explanations for his behavior.[15] Political scientist Michael P. Rogin, for example, argued in 1975 that Indian destruction was at the center of the American experience during the Age of Jackson. Allegedly the single figure most responsible for the carnage, Jackson is portrayed as an Indian-hater nonpareil whose monomania was the destruction of American Indians.[16]

According to Rogin's psychobiography of Old Hickory, anal and oral childhood difficulties helped to determine the course of Jackson's relations with Indians. In order to understand the president's behavior, *if* Rogin's analysis is correct, scholars need to study such elusive questions as Jackson's relationship with his mother (Rogin maintains that Jackson was uncertain whether he had "imbibed courage with his mother's milk") and his "anxieties over bodily control" (Rogin is particularly intrigued by Jackson's constant coughing, drooling, and constipation). The central thesis of Rogin's psychoanalytic study is that the subjugation of Indians helped Jackson to destroy his lingering fears of feminine domination and to grow securely to manhood. Most historians and political scientists, according to Rogin, have been "systematically deaf" to the familial language Jackson used in his dealings with the Indians, and Rogin urges them to probe for the hidden meaning of Jackson's references to Indians as "children" and to himself as their "Father."[17]

Many scholars have criticized Rogin's Freudian interpretation of Old Hickory's behavior for its "sweeping generalizations," its "tenuous historical judgments," and its "formula-ridden" approach.[18] Even before the publication of Rogin's psychobiography, the entire devil theory approach to the analysis of early-nineteenth-century Indian affairs had come under attack. A small number of historians argued that some of Jackson's contemporaries, including prominent clergymen and enlightened government officials, envisioned Indian removal as a means of rescuing eastern Indians from the evil effects of close contact with the advancing frontier. Herman J. Viola, the director of the National Anthropological Archives, summarized this revisionist position at a 1972 National Archives Conference on Indian-White Relations when he argued that "any fair appraisal of United States Indian policy in the period before the Civil War must take into consideration the genuine concern for the welfare and improvement of the Indians that existed among federal officials."[19]

Some of the revisionists have offered a reassessment of Jackson himself. They note that he adopted a Creek Indian orphan named Lincoyer and raised him at the Hermitage as his own son and point out other incidents in Old Hickory's life that do not support the stereotype of him as an Indian-hater. These historians have challenged the dualistic idea that the forces of evil led by Jackson supported Indian removal and that the forces of humanity opposed it. Certainly the president, a man of action and power, had many enemies who were eager to characterize him as a tyrant and a fiend. But as one critic of the devil theory has asked, "how often in history has there been someone all good or all evil?"[20]

The leading exponent of this revisionist interpretation is Marquette University historian Francis Paul Prucha. Since the late 1960s, Prucha has consistently argued that historians have paid too much attention to the rhetoric of Jackson's political adversaries and the less-than-disinterested Christian missionaries. Prucha's examination of Jackson's correspondence and speeches led him to conclude that Old Hickory did not have a doctrinaire anti-Indian attitude. According to Prucha, Old Hickory's dominant goal was to preserve the security and the prosperity of the United States and its white *and* Indian inhabitants. Prucha claims that a paternalistic interest in the Indians was pervasive in Jackson's thought and rhetoric as a military commander and later as president. He argues that Old Hickory's concern for the well-being and advancement of the Indians was genuine. Indeed Prucha equates Jackson's removal policy with efforts to "civilize" the Indians, and he concludes that the president had found a reasonable solution to the "Indian problem" confronting the United States.[21]

Prucha's revisionist interpretation, especially his emphasis on the sincerity of Jackson's humanitarian rhetoric, has created much controversy. Many scholars have refused to take his arguments seriously.[22] Some advocates of the devil theory, such as Ray Allen Billington and Robert V. Remini, however, have actually revised elements in their portrayal of Jackson's dealings with the Indians in order to accommodate Prucha's interpretation. Remini, for example, who in 1963 argued that Jackson had "a remarkable talent for slaughtering Indians" and that his concern for them "about equaled his affection for Henry Clay," was arguing in 1976 that Jackson was "most anxious to preserve Indian life and culture" and that he envisioned Indian removal as "the only way" to solve the "Indian problem." A year later Remini portrayed Jackson as a pragmatist who believed Indian removal was necessary to promote American expansion and security. Remini claimed that Indian removal "was not rape" but, essentially, "an exchange of land."[23]

Remini and revisionists such as Prucha are correct in noting that Jackson offered to pay Indians for their land and that he talked about removal in philanthropic terms, but until recently their accounts have tended to deemphasize important differences between the rhetoric of Old Hickory's Indian policy and the realities involved in executing the policy. Prucha has recently conceded that Jackson's Indian policy "had elements of good and evil, of humanitarian and philanthropic concern for the Indians and fraud and corruption practiced by unscrupulous men." Remini now concedes that while Jackson promised not to use coercion to win acceptance of his removal plan, he did indeed practice "a subtle kind of coercion." Unlike Michael Rogin, however, neither Remini nor Prucha views Jackson as an Indian-hater bent on the destruction of the Indian people.[24]

What were the realities of Jackson's Indian policy? Among those who witnessed the actual dispossession of the eastern tribes during Jackson's presidency was a French traveler who, while not an expert on Indian affairs, clearly recognized the deceptions involved in the treaty-making process. Alexis de Tocqueville poignantly observed that Jacksonian Indian policy was designed to evict the eastern tribes "with wonderful ease, quietly, legally, and philanthropically, without spilling blood and without violating a single one of the great principles of morality in the eyes of the world." According to Tocqueville, although American treaty commissioners, "inspired by the most chaste affection for legal formalities," used the treaty-making process and noble rhetoric to emphasize American justice in dealing with the Indians, the substance of American policy revealed manipulation and coercion. As Tocqueville concluded, "it is impossible to destroy men with more respect to the laws of humanity."[25]

Although the Jackson administration negotiated formal treaties with various tribes, paid them for their land cessions, and promised generous provisions for emigrants and those remaining behind, there were numerous defects in the treaty-making process. Treaty stipulations were provisional until formally ratified by the Senate, and delays in the ratification process often caused hardships for Indians awaiting promised supplies or funds. Americans rarely waited, however, for formal action by the Senate before moving into areas designated as Indian land cessions. Amended treaties had to be renegotiated with tribal leaders, but by the time this took place the Indians were frequently in a more unenviable bargaining position than they were originally. Moreover, the War Department blatantly violated tribal sovereignty by encouraging American treaty commissioners to *select* the particular chief or fraction of a tribe with whom the United States would deal or to whom the money for any ceded lands would be paid.[26] During the 1830s, for instance, commissioners slyly exploited the growing tribal divisions among the Cherokees and encouraged a minority faction to sign a removal treaty at New Echota in 1835 calling for the emigration of the *entire* Cherokee Nation.[27]

The fate of the southern Indians who chose to stay behind after the majority of their kinfolk emigrated to the West is also instructive. In order to secure the first treaty under the Removal Act, Jackson promised that any Indians wishing to remain in the East would receive land allotments and become citizens of the state in which they resided. The Choctaws signed a removal treaty in 1830. Jackson's rhetoric and the treaty pledges that echoed his promises were insufficient, however, to protect the six thousand Choctaws remaining in Mississippi after removal from the land hunger of white squatters and speculators who cheated them out of their allotments, homes, and other property. The treaty rights of these Indians were largely ignored by the Jackson administration and its successors, who found it politically expedient to leave them at the mercy of white Mississippians. Some Choctaws were "scourged, manacled, fettered and otherwise personally abused" by whites. Between the 1830s and 1918, when they were finally "rediscovered" by the federal government, the remnant of the Choctaws in Mississippi lived an existence worse than that of the average black in that state. Frauds committed by avaricious whites against the Choctaws embarrassed the Jackson administration, which later refused to provide similar allotments to the Cherokees. There was a marked contrast between Jackson's Indian policy, as outlined in the Removal Act of 1830 and described in his speeches, and the realities encountered by the Choctaws and Cherokees who remained behind after removal.[28]

Whatever the motive, conscious or unconscious, for the paternalistic language Jackson employed when talking with Indians and discussing his removal policy, the historical evidence clearly indicates that both the so-called devil and the revisionist or "angel" interpretations are too one-dimensional and simplistic. Andrew Jackson did not admire the ways of Indian life, but his views on Indian policy were shaped not so much by any ill will toward Indians as by his overwhelming concern for the growth, unity, and security of white America.

Before he became president, Jackson's relations with the Indians had been principally through his role as a military commander. In that role he eagerly recruited Indian allies and respected individual Indians. While he was a ruthless opponent in his campaigns against "hostile" Indians, he attacked all of his enemies (among others, the British, the Bank of the United States, and the South Carolina nullifiers) with the same ferocious zeal. His primary concern was for the material well-being, physical safety, and continuous expansion of white America.

Jackson certainly shared the ethnocentrism of his contemporaries and viewed efforts to transform the Indians into mirror images of white people as a positive and necessary step on the path from "savagism" to "civilization." If Old Hickory also believed his removal policy was in the best interests of the Indians, as revisionists such as Prucha claim, his assumption proved erroneous. Jackson was not, as Rogin and the advocates of the devil theory claim, driven by a hatred of the Indians that led him to commit genocide against them either. However, the methods he condoned to secure removal treaties and the actual implementation of his policy emasculated Indian sovereignty and brought many hardships to thousands of emigrants from numerous tribes who marched along trails of tears to the West, as well as to many of their kinfolk who stayed behind. While this suffering rebuts Remini's contention that "removal was not rape," the adaptive resiliency of the tribal societies and their histories after removal demonstrate the fallacy of Rogin's contention that "Death was the western tribal utopia" Jackson offered the Indians.[29]

For many years now, scholars of Jacksonian Indian policy have been too preoccupied with Old Hickory's attitude toward Indians and his motivation and too prone to view him as either a devil or an avenging angel. This tendency to see things in dualistic terms—good versus evil— is an old American characteristic. Anthropologist Edward T. Hall warned many years ago that "the ease with which Americans tend to polarize their thoughts about events may make it difficult for them to embrace an approach which employs three categories rather than two." Scholars of Indian-white relations, it would seem, are no exception to this generalization. As historian Oscar Handlin has noted, they have tended to ignore "the complexity and ambiguity of motives" involved in Indian removal and have too eagerly treated this episode in "simple good guys, bad [guys] fashion."[30] A more fruitful approach to understanding Jacksonian Indian policy than that of Prucha and Rogin, who have focused on the president's rhetoric as a key to understanding his motivation, may be to follow the old frontier maxim: "If you want to know what a politician is up to, watch his feet, not his mouth."[31]

How does Old Hickory's rhetoric compare with his actions and the results of his policy? Jackson and his administrative staff in the War Department and the Indian Office maintained that the removal policy would bring at least four major benefits to the Indians. These were (1) fixed and permanent boundaries outside the jurisdiction of American states and territories, (2) isolation from corrupt white elements, (3) tribal self-government unfettered by state or territorial laws, and (4) opportunities to acquire the essentials of "civilized" society (Christianity, private property, and knowledge of agriculture and the mechanical arts). The rhetoric of Jackson's policy emphasized its philanthropic goals, but neither the president nor anyone else in his administration was willing to undertake adequate long-range planning or to commit the federal government to undertake more responsibilities for, or to spend more money on, the Indians than was absolutely necessary. Throughout the Jacksonian era, retrenchment in government expenditures was a tenet of good government, and the exigencies of the moment actually determined the components of the removal policy.[32]

Was the removal policy a success in terms of the four alleged benefits that Jackson claimed it would bring the Indians after their relocation? In his great rush to enact the Indian Removal Bill, Jackson and his congressional supporters seemed unconcerned about the technical aspects of any subsequent migration of thousands of eastern Indians to the trans-Mississippi West. Opponents of the bill in Congress had raised several important questions: Would emigration be purely voluntary? Would treaty commissioners negotiate only with acknowledged tribal leaders or would land be purchased from individuals? How many Indians would go? What kind of preparations and resources would be necessary for them? What would be the specific boundaries between emigrant tribes? How would the indigenous tribes in the West react to the intrusion of new people?[33] Despite these questions concerning the welfare of Indian emigrants, only in 1832, long after the first emigrants had arrived in the West, did the Jackson administration take steps to provide a plan for "their improvement, government, and security." These measures came at a time when the hardships being suffered by the Choctaws, the first tribe to emigrate west under the terms of the Removal Act, were making it difficult for the president to secure Senate ratification of additional removal treaties with other southern tribes, particularly the Cherokee.[34]

The Removal Act had authorized President Jackson to exchange unorganized public domain in the trans-Mississippi West for Indian landholdings in the East and to assure emigrant Indians that "the United States will forever secure and guaranty to them, and their heirs or successors, the country so exchanged with them." As mentioned earlier, the Choctaw treaty of 1830 included such an exchange and guarantee. While Choctaw emigrants were en route to the West in 1831, however, Jackson decided that a portion of the land recently assigned to them there was needed for the Chickasaws. Anxious to open Chickasaw lands in Mississippi and Alabama to white settlement, the president sent the negotiators of the Choctaw treaty to "effect an arrangement" whereby a portion of the new Choctaw lands in the West would be made available to the Chickasaws. One of the Choctaws who met with the American treaty negotiators to discuss Jackson's proposal reflected the views of many others when he suggested the president should at least allow the Indians to step on the soil of their new tribal domain before asking them to sell a part of it.[35]

As a result of the Choctaw experience, Cherokee Chief John Ross and the leaders of other southern tribes had good reasons to be skeptical when Jackson's treaty negotiators promised them land in the West "forever." These Indians and their white allies realized "forever" actually did not mean for all time but rather only for as long as it suited the interests of white people.

Although the Jackson administration was anxious to relocate the major southern tribes in the area west of the Arkansas-Missouri line, it did not direct all the northern Indians to the region designated as Indian country by the Removal Act. Jackson, whose primary concern in Indian affairs was the removal of the southern tribes, was willing to take a more piecemeal approach to the removal of northern Indians. Whenever the exigencies of the moment demanded it, Jackson (and later his successors) acted.[36]

Some northern Indians avoided eviction to the West, but others suffered the hardships of removal more than once. The Winnebagos in what is today southwestern and south central Wisconsin eventually ceded land in seven different treaties involving *six* possible changes in residence between 1829 and 1866. While the Jackson administration was pushing the Winnebagos farther west to free them from the alleged evils of close contact with whites, it was also fulfilling old treaty stipulations and seeking new ones to settle various New York tribes in Wisconsin. During the 1830s, both the indigenous tribes in southern Wisconsin and the resettled New York Indians, who were viewed as exploitive interlopers by the former, felt the pressures of the great land boom that swept the region and faced the prospect of future removals.[37]

The Jackson administration also failed to undertake long-range planning for the establishment of permanent boundaries in the West for the Potawatomis who ceded their lands in the Lake Michigan area in 1833. The new Potawatomi lands included the Platte country, a region that Congress was already targeting for incorporation into the state of Missouri. Although spoken at a later time, the words of Sioux Chief Spotted Tail summarize the reality facing Winnebago and Potawatomi emigrants: "Why does not the Great Father put his red children on wheels, so he can move them as he will?" Contrary to Jackson's philanthropic rhetoric, removal did not bring all emigrants fixed and permanent boundaries outside the jurisdiction of American states and territories; federal officials were more responsive to the needs of state and territorial leaders and white citizens than to Indians claiming their treaty rights.[38]

The second alleged benefit of removal was isolation from corrupt white elements. In 1834, President Jackson advocated the enactment of legislation to protect the Indians from land-hungry whites, whiskey peddlers, and other troublesome Americans. Nothing, including Indian treaty rights, however, stopped the advance of white settlement, and the traffic in "ardent spirits" continued. Moreover, the Trade and Intercourse Act of 1834 directly contradicted Jackson's third promise, that the Indians could pursue self-rule in the West. The act specified that American laws would take precedence over Indian laws and customs in all cases involving Indians and whites and, thereby, left Indians accused of crimes against whites at the mercy of law-enforcement agents and courts in white communities adjoining Indian settlements.[39] Finally, the War Department interfered in tribal affairs by openly playing "Indian politics" and encouraging agents to use the distribution of funds owed the Indians to manipulate tribal leaders.[40]

Jackson's fourth promise was that the federal government would promote the "civilization" of the Indians in the West. Although his administration supported educational programs for the emigrant tribes in the West, these efforts, part of the so-called Civilization Program that had evolved years earlier, were designed to essentially transform Indians into mirror images of white people. Such programs stressed acculturation rather than assimilation, and despite the sympathetic attitude of individual missionaries and other white teachers, they were too often merely a convenient means of undermining Indian culture and controlling tribal societies. Although it is patently unfair to expect early-nineteenth-century white Americans to have approached the Indians with the cultural relativity of twentieth-century anthropologists, the prevailing ethnocentrism of the Jacksonian era meant that even acculturation could not guarantee Indians equality in white society.[41]

Whether nefarious, noble, or simply pragmatic considerations lay behind Jackson's Indian policy is an issue that made little difference to the Indian people who felt its effects. Although Jackson maintained in his farewell address in 1837 that removal to the West had finally placed eastern Indians "beyond the reach of injury or oppression, and that the paternal care of the General Government will hereafter watch over them and protect them,"[42] there were plenty of Indian skeptics. The clarion call of manifest destiny during the 1840s led many "sincere and disinterested friends of the Indians" to wonder if the existing treaties with emigrant tribes in the West would be upheld "or, whether those treaties are to be set at naught . . . and the red race again be driven and dispersed." The historical record clearly indicates there was a wide gap between Old Hickory's rhetoric and the actual results of his Indian policy. Historians must not ignore this gap, but neither should they assume its existence alone explains the fate of the Indian people in the 1830s.[43]

Jackson was certainly the most prominent advocate of Indian removal, and he condoned the use of bribery and brute force to promote emigration. Indian affairs, however, was not his primary concern as president. Historian Richard B. Latner, for example, asserts that "it is questionable whether Jackson ever accorded Indian affairs the centrality that he gave his monetary and banking policies."[44] Many people actually shouldered the burden of putting the removal policy into effect and supplying information to help officials in Washington make their decisions. Indeed there was a remarkable diffusion of decision-making authority in Indian affairs and in other areas of public administration in the 1830s because the nature of the problems necessitated a sharing of power. Therefore, the implementation of federal Indian policy ultimately depended on the character, integrity, intelligence, and interests of scattered field officials and the willingness of frontier law-enforcement agencies and judicial systems to find whites guilty when arrested for crimes against Indians.[45] Thus, by focusing their attention either on an alleged pathology of President Jackson or on his supposed humanitarianism, scholars have deemphasized or ignored many very important aspects of Indian-white relations.

Much of the suffering actually encountered by emigrating Indians in the 1830s was the result of the excesses of partisan politics and the prevailing belief that retrenchment and good government were synonymous. The policy of issuing contracts for food and transportation for emigrants to the lowest bidders contributed to the misery of Indians on their trek to the West more than anything else. Many unscrupulous contractors furnished the emigrants with scanty, even spoiled rations, thin blankets, and other shoddy items in order to reap a sizable profit from their contracts. Contractors were businessmen out to make a profit, and they were quite successful. Efforts to economize in removal expenditures by speeding up the movement of Indians also led to much suffering. Ironically, such efforts were often in response to critics of Indian removal such as Henry Clay, who while opposing the policy on supposedly humanitarian grounds, also complained that it cost too much. These opponents were at least partially responsible for the continued use of the bidding system and the frugality that characterized federal Indian policy.[46]

Scholars should not assume that the Indians would necessarily have fared better under Jackson's political opponents. Neither Democrat nor Whig politicians doubted the superiority of American culture, the desirability of "civilizing" the Indians, or the need for allegedly "higher uses" of Indian lands. Throughout the 1830s, leaders in both major political parties focused their attention on partisan politics, patronage, and retrenchment to the detriment of the administration of Indian affairs and the welfare of the Indian people. In 1838, Sen. Daniel Webster lamented the lack of "public sympathies" for the "base fraud" committed against the Cherokee Nation by the ratification of the controversial Treaty of New Echota two years earlier. "The Whig members of Congress, who have taken an interest in seeing justice done to the Indians, are worn out and exhausted," he noted, adding that "an Administration man, come from where he will, had no concern for Indian rights." Whig leaders certainly condemned aspects of Jackson's Indian policy, but when their party captured the White House in 1840, they continued the policy.[47] In terms of their relations with whites, the real problem confronting the Indians between 1829 and 1837 was not simply the presence of Jackson in the White House, but that, as one astute contemporary put it, "the whole Indian race" was not, "in the political scales, worth one white man's vote."[48]

It was more than coincidental that the great era of Indian removal occurred during the period generally associated with the achievement of political democracy in America—the so-called Age of the Common Man —and that it was Andrew Jackson, often called the symbol for the era, who promoted the eviction of the Indians.[49] Jackson was a product of his times, and his beliefs, though perhaps distinguished by their intensity, were similar to those of many of his contemporaries. As historian Henry Fritz argues, because of the egocentric nature of people, "political democracy has always best served the interests of powerful groups, and has neglected weak minorities."[50]

The United States in the Jacksonian era increasingly became a market-focused society dominated by expectant capitalists, and federal officials were under unremitting pressure to remove all impediments to the exploitation of the nation's natural resources. Men of all political persuasions sought the immense tracts of valuable land, virgin forests, and mineral reserves located in Indian country within the United States. During this period, the equation of Indian removal with the preservation and "civilization" of the Indians often served as a convenient humanitarian rationale for the dispossession of Indian people. Notable historians, scientists, and literary figures were among the majority who pitied the plight of the Indians but acknowledged that they had to make way for "progress." The rise of scientific racism in the 1830s led white Americans to emphasize race and to deemphasize other factors, including environment and culture, in explaining the differences between themselves and Indians, whom they assumed to be a doomed race. Furthermore, because of the self-interested orientation of public opinion, few Americans voiced concern about the discrepancies between the benevolent rhetoric and the frequently cruel realities of American Indian policy.[51]

Such discrepancies bothered white friends of the Indians and were frequently decried by foreign visitors. In the early 1830s, for example, the English traveler Frances Trollope charged that Jackson's removal policy epitomized everything despicable in American character, especially the "contradictions in their principles and practice." Trollope viewed Indian removal as a "treacherous policy" that demonstrated the true character of the American people. "You will see them one hour lecturing their mob on the indefeasible rights of man," she wrote, "and the next driving from their homes the children of the soil, whom they have bound themselves to protect by the most solemn treaties."[52]

Several years later, geologist George Featherstonhaugh witnessed firsthand the results of the policy Trollope had condemned. In 1837, this scientist, an Englishman who had lived in the United States for nearly thirty years, traveled through the Cherokee country in the South. Although Jackson was no longer president, his handpicked successor, Martin Van Buren, had made clear his determination to enforce the controversial Cherokee removal treaty of 1835. Featherstonhaugh was impressed by the remarkable advances the Cherokees had made in the "great principles of civilization." All about him he saw signs of progress—the presence of Christian missionaries and churches, books printed in the native language, a tribal government based on written laws, and fields under cultivation. He lamented that the Cherokees were being "driven from their religious and social state . . . not because they cannot be civilized, but because a pseudo set of civilized beings, who are too strong for them, want their possessions!" Featherstonhaugh shared Trollope's contempt for the "wrongful manner" by which Americans acquired Indian lands.[53]

As the observations of Trollope and Featherstonhaugh suggest, the contrast between the rhetoric and the reality of President Jackson's Indian policy serves as a grim reminder of what can happen to a politically powerless minority in a democratic society. Scholars of Indian-white relations would be wise, however, to heed the advice of Edward Hall and Oscar Handlin and avoid thinking about the Jacksonian Indian policy in dualistic terms. An analysis of the reasons for the differences between the rhetoric and the reality of Jacksonian Indian policy also points out the danger of oversimplified, one-dimensional interpretations of history.

NOTES

1. Edward Pessen, *Jacksonian America: Society, Personality, and Politics*, rev. ed. (Homewood, Ill.: Dorsey Press, 1978), 1.

2. For the dimensions of the debate on Jackson's relations with the Indian tribes at the time this paper was presented at the Cherokee Removal Conference co-sponsored by Western Carolina University and the Museum of the Cherokee Indian in April 1986, see Francis Paul Prucha, "Andrew Jackson's Indian Policy: A Reassessment," *Journal of American History* 56 (December 1969): 527–39; Ronald N. Satz, *American Indian Policy in the Jacksonian Era* (Lincoln: University of Nebraska Press, 1975); Michael Paul Rogin, *Fathers and Children: Andrew Jackson and the Subjugation of the American Indian* (New York: Alfred A. Knopf, 1975); Ronald N. Satz, "Indian Policy in the Jacksonian Era: The Old Northwest as a Test Case," *Michigan History* 60 (Spring 1976), 71–93; Robert V. Remini, *Andrew Jackson*, 3 vols. (New York: Harper and Row, 1977–84), 1:321–98, 2:257–79, 3:293–314; and Francis Paul Prucha, *The Great Father: The United States Government and the American Indians*, 2 vols. (Lincoln: University of Nebraska Press, 1984): 1:191ff. For a more detailed analysis of the issues discussed in this essay, see the revised edition of *American Indian Policy in the Jacksonian Era*, which is forthcoming from the University of Oklahoma Press. (Citations in this essay to pages from *American Indian Policy in the Jacksonian Era* refer to the first edition.)

3. Maps detailing all Indian land cessions during this period are available in Charles C. Royce, comp., *Indian Land Cessions in the United States* (1900; reprint, New York: Arno Press and The New York Times, 1971). For the treaties, see Charles J. Kappler, comp. and ed., *Indian Affairs: Laws and Treaties*, 5 vols. (Washington, D.C.: Government Printing Office, 1909–41), 2:297–489.

4. Satz, *American Indian Policy in the Jacksonian Era*, 9–31; *Statutes at Large of the United States of America, 1789–1873*, 17 vols. (Washington, D.C., 1850–73), 4:411–12. For a general history of Indian removal before Jackson's presidency, see Annie H. Abel, "The History of Events Resulting in Indian Consolidation West of the Mississippi," *Annual Report of the American Historical Association for the Year 1906*, 2 vols. (Washington, D.C.: Government Printing Office, 1908), 1:241–370.

5. *Report of the Commissioner of Indian Affairs*, 24th Cong., 2d sess., December 1,

1836, S. Doc. 1, 420; Statement of the General Land Office, August 8, 1836, Statement Showing the Number of Indians, December 1, 1836, and Statement Showing the Quantity of Lands Ceded by the Indian Tribes to the United States, December 1, 1836, Office of Indian Affairs, Miscellaneous Records, 1:300–1, 2:6–8, 90–92, 98–100, Record Group 75, National Archives, Washington, D.C. According to the Indian Office records cited here, only about 9,000 Indians, mostly in the Old Northwest and New York, were without treaty stipulations requiring their removal. There is evidence to indicate, however, that the number of such Indians was much larger than the Indian Office reported. The dearth of reliable population statistics on Indians during the Jacksonian era is a perplexing problem for scholars, but there were probably more than 9,000 Indians without treaties requiring removal in Wisconsin Territory alone at this time. See Alice E. Smith, *The History of Wisconsin*, vol. 1, *From Exploration to Statehood* (Madison: State Historical Society of Wisconsin, 1973), 129 n. 7.

6. In the introduction to his edition of *Cherokee Removal: The "William Penn" Essays and Other Writings of Jeremiah Evarts* (Knoxville: University of Tennessee Press, 1979), Francis Paul Prucha asserts that the removal issue was "a question that agitated the nation to its very roots, in the press and on the floor of Congress, and it touched the fundamental conception of the United States as a Christian nation" (p. 3). Robert V. Remini, however, claims that "there was no public outcry against it. In fact it was hardly noticed" (*Andrew Jackson* 2:265).

7. For Jackson's position, see James D. Richardson, comp., *A Compilation of the Messages and Papers of the Presidents,* 10 vols. (Washington, D.C.: Government Printing Office, 1896–99), 2:438, 456–59, 519–23, 536–41, 554–55, 565–66, 597, 3:32–33, 171–73, 294 (hereafter cited as *Compilation of Messages*). The quotations are from ibid. 2:522, and Jackson to Capt. James Gadsen, October 12, 1829, in *Correspondence of Andrew Jackson,* ed. John Spencer Bassett, 7 vols. (Washington, D.C.: Carnegie Institution, 1926–35), 4:81.

8. Marie P. Mahoney, "American Public Opinion of Andrew Jackson's Indian Policy, 1828–1835" (master's thesis, Clark University, 1935); Carol A. Kurtz, "Public Opinion and Andrew Jackson's Indian Removal Program" (master's thesis, Columbia University, 1963); Richard B. Latner, *The Presidency of Andrew Jackson: White House Politics, 1829–1837* (Athens: University of Georgia Press, 1979), 92; David J. Russo, *The Major Political Issues of the Jacksonian Period and the Development of Party Loyalty in Congress, 1830–1840, Transactions of the American Philosophical Society,* n.s., vol. 62, pt. 5 (Philadelphia, 1972), 13–14. Francis Paul Prucha claims that "the hue and cry raised against removal" was largely politically inspired ("Andrew Jackson's Indian Policy," 538). For the political response to the Removal Act, see Satz, *American Indian Policy in the Jacksonian Era,* 39–56.

9. Samuel Flagg Bemis, *John Quincy Adams and the Foundations of American Foreign Policy* (New York: Alfred A. Knopf, 1949), 201, 208; *Memoirs of John Quincy Adams*, ed. Charles Francis Adams, 12 vols. (Philadelphia: J. B. Lippincott, 1874–77), 7:90; Carl Schurz, *Life of Henry Clay*, 2 vols. (Boston: Houghton Mifflin, 1887), 2:59; Clement Eaton, *Henry Clay and the Art of American Politics* (Boston: Little, Brown, 1957), 115–17.

10. U.S. Congress, *Register of Debates in Congress*, 21st Cong., 1st sess., 307, 309–20, 380–81, 383; Theodore Frelinghuysen to Jeremiah Evarts, January 11, February 22, March 7, 1830, Evarts Family Papers, Sterling Memorial Library, Yale University, New Haven, Conn.; Charles R. Erdman, Jr., "Theodore Frelinghuysen," in *Dictionary of American Biography*, ed. Allen Johnson and Dumas Malone, 22 vols. (New York: Charles Scribner's Sons, 1956), 7:16; Theodore Frelinghuysen to Jeremiah Evarts, February 1, 1830, Evarts Papers, Library of Congress, Washington, D.C.; Clifford S. Griffin, "Religious Benevolence as Social Control, 1815–1860," *Mississippi Valley Historical Review* 44 (December 1957): 423–44. Also see [Jeremiah Evarts] to David Greene, March 31, 1830, American Board of Commissioners for Foreign Missions Papers, Houghton Library, Harvard University, Cambridge, Mass.

11. As John William Ward noted, "Andrew Jackson's opponents saw his relation to nature as that of the savage; Jackson's name was synonymous with barbarism" (*Andrew Jackson: Symbol for an Age* [New York: Oxford University Press, 1962], 43). Also see Robert F. Berkhofer, Jr., *The White Man's Indian: Images of the American Indian from Columbus to the Present* (New York: Alfred A. Knopf, 1978), 161–62. For the debates on the removal bill, see *Register of Debates in Congress*, 21st Cong., 1st sess., 305ff, 580ff (February 24, 1830, and following, in the House of Representatives, and April 6, 1830, and following, in the Senate). The speeches against the bill were edited by Jeremiah Evarts under the title *Speeches on the Passage of the Bill, for the Removal of the Indians, Delivered in the Congress of the United States, April and May, 1830* (Boston: Perkins and Marvin, 1830). Also see [Jeremiah Evarts], *Essays on the Present Crisis in the Condition of the American Indians; First Published in the National Intelligencer, under the Signature of William Penn* (Boston: Perkins and Marvin, 1829).

12. For citations to historical studies that follow the devil theory approach, see Francis Paul Prucha, "Indian Removal and the Great American Desert," *Indiana Magazine of History* 59 (December 1963): 300–301n; Prucha, "Andrew Jackson's Indian Policy," 527n; Bernard W. Sheehan, "Indian-White Relations in Early America: A Review Essay," *William and Mary Quarterly*, 3d ser., 26 (April 1969): 281–82n; Richard H. Faust, "Another Look at General Jackson and the Indians of the Mississippi Territory," *Alabama Review* 28 (July 1975): 202n.

13. The following are examples of scholars who claim that removal was obligatory under the 1830 legislation: Charles Hudson, *The Southeastern Indians* (Knoxville: University of Tennessee Press, 1976), 455; James A. Clifton, *The Prairie People: Continuity and Change in Potawatomi Indian Culture, 1665–1965* (Lawrence: Regents Press of Kansas, 1977), 257; Alvin M. Josephy, Jr., *On the Hill: A History of the American Congress, from 1789 to the Present* (New York: Simon and Schuster, 1979), 171; William Appleman Williams, *Empire as a Way of Life: An Essay on the Causes and Character of America's Present Predicament Along with a Few Thoughts About an Alternative* (New York: Oxford University Press, 1980), 83; Arrel Morgan Gibson, *The American Indian: Prehistory to the Present* (Lexington, Mass.: D. C. Heath, 1980), 309. Ethnologist Peter Farb's *Ma's Rise to Civilization as Shown by the Indians of North America from Primeval Times to the Coming of the Industrial State* (New York: E. P. Dutton, 1968), a popular Book of the Month Club selection in the late 1960s, claims that Jackson "exerted his influence to make Congress give legal sanction to what in our own time, under the Nuremburg Laws, would be branded as genocide. Dutifully, Congress passed the Removal Act of 1830, which gave the President the right to extirpate all Indians who had managed to survive east of the Mississippi River" (p. 250). At a session titled "The Writing of American Indian History" at the Seventy-third Annual Meeting of the Organization of American Historians in San Francisco, Roxanne Dunbar Ortiz argued that "the *policy* of genocide on the part of the United States government was very real" during the Jacksonian era ("Comments," furnished by the author, 1980, p. 9 [italics in original]). For the actual wording of the Removal Act, see *Statutes at Large* 4:411–12.

14. Ronald T. Takaki, *Iron Cages: Race and Culture in Nineteenth-Century America* (New York: Alfred A. Knopf, 1979), 100, 103, 106, 107.

15. The leading examples are Rogin, *Fathers and Children,* and James C. Curtis, *Andrew Jackson and the Search for Vindication* (Boston: Little, Brown, 1976).

16. Rogin, *Fathers and Children,* passim. Also see Rogin's "Indian Extinction, American Regeneration," *Journal of Ethnic Studies* 2 (Spring 1974): 93–102, and "Liberal Society and the Indian Question," *Politics and Society* 1 (May 1971): 269–312.

17. Rogin, *Fathers and Children,* 12, 129, 285.

18. This statement is based on a thorough examination of all reviews of Rogin's book listed in *Book Review Index* from 1975 to 1980. The quotations are from Herman J. Viola's review in *Pacific Historical Review* 47 (May 1978): 296, and Robert McColley's review in *Journal of American History* 62 (March 1976): 990–91. Also see Edwin A. Miles, "Forty-second Annual Meeting of the Southern Historical Association," *Journal of Southern History* 43 (February 1977): 87–88. Elsewhere I have argued that "Rogin qualifies many of his statements with a 'perhaps' or a 'may have.' Yet he ignores these qualifiers when he draws his conclusions and, thereby,

forecloses alternative hypotheses. There are serious problems involved in examining the human psyche to achieve a comprehensive analysis of motivation when the subject is dead and only traces of his personality can be analyzed. Not only is there no one accepted theory of human motivation today, but even the demonstrated existence of a recognizable pathology may not necessarily explain all of an individual's actions." See Ronald N. Satz, review of *Fathers and Children*, by Michael P. Rogin, *American Historical Review* 81 (June 1976): 658–59. For reactions to Rogin's interpretation that discuss the problems of writing psychohistory, see Martin H. Quitt, "Jackson, Indians, and Psychohistory," *History of Childhood Quarterly* 3 (Spring 1976): 543–51, and Lewis Perry, review of *Fathers and Children*, *History and Theory* 16 (May 1977): 174–95.

19. Herman J. Viola, "From Civilization to Removal: Early American Indian Policy," in *National Archives Conferences*, vol. 10, *Indian-White Relations: A Persistent Paradox*, ed. Jane F. Smith and Robert M. Kvasnicka (Washington, D.C.: Howard University Press, 1976), 45. For examples of the scholarship mentioned above, see Francis Paul Prucha, *American Indian Policy in the Formative Years: The Indian Trade and Intercourse Acts, 1790–1834* (Cambridge: Harvard University Press, 1962), 231–49; Francis Paul Prucha, *Lewis Cass and American Indian Policy* (Detroit: Wayne State University Press, 1967); Frederick M. Binder, *The Color Problem in Early National America as Viewed by John Adams, Jefferson, and Jackson* (The Hague: Mouton, 1968), 152–54, 156; Sheehan, "Indian-White Relations," 267–86; Prucha, "Andrew Jackson's Indian Policy," 527–39; George A. Schultz, *An Indian Canaan: Isaac McCoy and the Vision of an Indian State* (Norman: University of Oklahoma Press, 1972); Bernard W. Sheehan, *Seeds of Extinction: Jeffersonian Philanthropy and the American Indian* (Chapel Hill: University of North Carolina Press, 1973); Herman J. Viola, *Thomas L. McKenney: Architect of America's Early Indian Policy, 1816–1830* (Chicago: Swallow Press, 1974); W. Eugene Hollon, *Frontier Violence: Another Look* (New York: Oxford University Press, 1974), 202–17. Also see Francis Paul Prucha, ed., *The Indian in American History* (New York: Holt, Rinehart and Winston, 1971), 3–4.

20. See Prucha, "Andrew Jackson's Indian Policy," 527–39; Binder, *Color Problem*, 152–54, 156; and Faust, "Another Look at General Jackson," 202–17 (quotation p. 217).

21. Holman Hamilton, "The Sixty-first Annual Meeting of the Organization of American Historians," *Journal of American History* 55 (September 1968): 351–52; Prucha, "Andrew Jackson's Indian Policy," 527–39. Also see Prucha's "The Image of the Indian in Pre–Civil War America," in *Indiana Historical Society Lectures, 1970–1971: American Indian Policy* (Indianapolis: Indiana Historical Society, 1971), 3–16; and his "Indians and Whites: Assimilation or Segregation," in *Main Problems in American History*, ed. Howard H. Quint et al., 4th ed., 2 vols. (Homewood, Ill.: Dorsey Press, 1978), 1:226–27.

22. Edward Pessen, for example, describes Prucha's 1969 revisionist article, "Andrew Jackson's Indian Policy," as "standing in lonely splendor in its favorable appraisal of Jacksonian policy." Pessen finds the article "altogether unconvincing, if reflective of the gentlemanly traits of its author" (*Jacksonian America*, 361). Commenting on Prucha's *American Indian Policy in the Formative Years*, Wilcomb E. Washburn asserts that "the question of motive in philanthropic activities relating to the Indian is a critical issue. I have in recent years, debated the question of governmental motivation with Father Paul Prucha and I would like to restate the issue in the following way. Prucha (1962), and many others, give what seems to me excessive credit for motives which are expressed intentions but which seem to me to lack the degree of integrity required to make one accept them at full faith. Prucha seems to me to tell the formal story of federal policy in this period without always telling the real story. It is essentially a history of Indian policy from the viewpoint of the Washington administrator with too infrequent reference or relation to what was actually happening in 'the field.' One thinks of the futility of analyzing Spanish Indian policy in terms of the *Laws of the Indies*. The disparity between form and reality is not so great in the American case, but its significance is too frequently overlooked by the historian" ("Philanthropy and the American Indian: The Need for a Model," *Ethnohistory* 15 [Winter 1968]: 54). In 1975, however, Washburn conceded some points to Prucha and concluded that the removal policy "cannot readily be dismissed either as a failure or a success, as malevolent or benevolent. It partakes of both." See *The Indian in America* (New York: Harper and Row, 1975), 167–69.

23. Compare Billington's *Westward Expansion: A History of the American Frontier*, 3d ed. (New York: Macmillan, 1967), 314–15, and 4th ed. (New York: Macmillan, 1974), 301–2. For Remini's changing views, see *The Election of Andrew Jackson* (Philadelphia: J. B. Lippincott, 1963), 13, 75; *Andrew Jackson* (New York: Twayne Publishers, 1966), 117; *The Age of Jackson* (New York: Harper and Row, 1972), 63; *The Revolutionary Age of Andrew Jackson* (New York: Harper and Row, 1976), 111; *Andrew Jackson* 1:336 (1977).

24. Prucha, *Great Father* 1:181; Remini, *Andrew Jackson* 2:264. See "Remini's Andrew Jackson (1767–1821): Andrew Jackson and the Indians," *Tennessee Historical Quarterly* 38 (Summer 1979): 158–66, for my criticism of Remini's first volume of *Andrew Jackson* (1977), which was originally presented at the Forty-fourth Annual Meeting of the Southern Historical Association in 1978. For Remini's response, see *Andrew Jackson* 2:257–79 (chap. 15).

25. Alexis de Tocqueville, *Democracy in America*, ed. J. P. Mayer, trans. George Lawrence (Garden City, N.Y.: Anchor Books, 1969), 339. Published originally in 1835 and translated into English in 1838, Tocqueville's book contains a section titled "The Present State and the Probable Future of the Indian Tribes Inhabiting the

Territory of the Union" (see pp. 321–39). Two articles by Gary C. Stein examine what Tocqueville and other European visitors thought of American-Indian relations; see "'And the Strife Never Ends': Indian-White Hostility as Seen by European Travelers in America, 1800–1860," *Ethnohistory* 20 (Spring 1973): 173–85, and "Indian Removal as Seen by European Travelers in America," *Chronicles of Oklahoma* 51 (Winter 1973–74): 399–410.

26. See Satz, *American Indian Policy in the Jacksonian Era*, 64–145, 211–36, and Satz, "Indian Policy in the Jacksonian Era," 71–93.

27. For two different perspectives on Cherokee factionalism in the 1830s, see Gary E. Moulton, *John Ross: Cherokee Chief* (Athens: University of Georgia Press, 1978), 50–126, and Thurman Wilkins, *Cherokee Tragedy: The Ridge Family and the Decimation of a People*, 2d ed., rev. (Norman: University of Oklahoma Press, 1986), 214–339.

28. Ronald N. Satz, "The Mississippi Choctaw: From the Removal Treaty to the Federal Agency," in *After Removal: The Choctaw in Mississippi*, ed. Samuel J. Wells and Roseanna Tubby (Jackson: University Press of Mississippi, 1986), 3–32. The quotation is from "Petition of One Hundred Red Men," December 6, 1849, Office of Indian Affairs, Choctaw Emigration, Letters Received, Record Group 75, National Archives. For the treatment of Indians in the South after the removal era, see Walter L. Williams, ed., *Southeastern Indians Since the Removal Era* (Athens: University of Georgia Press, 1979). The allotment policy is ably discussed in Mary E. Young, *Redskins, Ruffleshirts, and Rednecks: Indian Allotments in Alabama and Mississippi, 1830–1860* (Norman: University of Oklahoma Press, 1961), and Paul W. Gates, "Indian Allotments Preceding the Dawes Act," in *The Frontier Challenge: Responses to the Trans-Mississippi West*, ed. John G. Clark (Lawrence: University Press of Kansas, 1971), 141–67. For information on the Cherokee efforts to secure allotments and their condition in the East after removal, see John R. Finger, *The Eastern Band of Cherokees, 1819–1900* (Knoxville: University of Tennessee Press, 1984).

29. This and the preceding two paragraphs are based on my *American Indian Policy in the Jacksonian Era;* "Indian Policy in the Jacksonian Era," 71–93; review of *Fathers and Children*, by Michael P. Rogin, 658–59; and "Remini's Andrew Jackson," 158–66. The Remini quotation is from *Andrew Jackson* 1:336; the Rogin quotation is from *Fathers and Children*, 245. For examples of the resiliency of native American tribal societies after removal, see Angie Debo, *A History of the Indians of the United States* (Norman: University of Oklahoma Press, 1979), 128, and Gibson, *American Indian*, 338–41. Scholars often discuss Jackson's Indian policy in terms of a generalized or stereotyped Indian. But, in actuality, specific Indian groups in particular environments interacted with certain white Americans, and the results were not always the same. Some native groups avoided removal and do not neatly fit the

so-called Jacksonian pattern. For information on southern Indians who avoided removal and the remnants of the removed tribes, see Williams, ed., *Southeastern Indians Since the Removal Era,* 27–207. Although there is no comparable study of the northern Indians, useful information about the individual tribes is provided in Bruce G. Trigger, ed., *Northeast,* vol. 15 of *Handbook of North American Indians,* ed. William Sturtevant (Washington, D.C.: Smithsonian Institution, 1978); also see *Report of the Commissioner of Indian Affairs,* 33d Cong., 1st sess., November 26, 1853, S. Exec. Doc. 1, 243.

30. Edward T. Hall, *The Silent Language* (New York: Doubleday, 1959), 65–66; Oscar Handlin, *Truth in History* (Cambridge: Harvard University Press, Belknap Press, 1979), 397–98. Handlin bemoans the "victimization" approach to the writing of Indian history and the "atonement books" that have appeared in recent years. For references to what he refers to as "judicious and unsensational books" on nineteenth-century Indian affairs that "had no hope" of winning popular attention, see Handlin, *Truth in History,* 399 n. 21.

31. Quoted in Marvin Meyers, *The Jacksonian Persuasion: Politics and Belief* (New York: Vintage Books, 1960), v. According to Meyers, "To watch the politician's feet is to learn how the public business is dispatched from day to day, especially when nerves are relaxed and public attention diffused. To attend to political talk is to learn how politicians justify their arrangements for the common good when the public, in ages of tension and distress, recovers the original sense that this is a nation with a purpose and demands an accounting. The best public talk is no more than prudence—as much of political truth as available leaders can handle and the public can bear. The worst is beneath contempt. The Jacksonian persuasion lies somewhere between" (ibid., ix).

32. See n. 7, above. Also see Satz, *American Indian Policy in the Jacksonian Era,* and Satz, "Indian Policy in the Jacksonian Era," 71–93.

33. For the debate on the bill, see *Register of Debates in Congress,* 21st Cong., 1st sess., 305ff and 580ff (February 24, 1830, and following, in the House of Representatives, and April 6, 1830, and following, in the Senate). The speeches against the bill were reprinted; see Evarts, ed., *Speeches on the Passage of the Bill, for the Removal of the Indians.*

34. *Statutes at Large* 4:595–96; Lewis Cass to Maj. J. W. Flowers, May 24, 1832, *Correspondence on the Subject of the Emigration of Indians,* 23d Cong., 1st sess., S. Doc. 512, 2:839; Isaac McCoy's Private Journal, March 28, August 27, 1832, Isaac McCoy Papers, Kansas State Historical Society, Topeka, Kans.; *Warrenton Reporter* (North Carolina), November 1, 1832; Lewis Cass to Commissioners, July 14, 1832, Office of Indian Affairs, Letters Sent, 9:33–40, Record Group 75, National Archives; Satz, *American Indian Policy in the Jacksonian Era,* 79, 126–35.

35. *Statutes at Large* 4:411–12; Kappler, comp. and ed., *Indian Affairs,* 2:310–

11; John Coffee to Lewis Cass, August 21, 1831, Office of Indian Affairs, Choctaw Agency Emigration, Letters Received, Record Group 75, National Archives; Andrew Jackson to Secretary of War, October 18, 1831, Levi Woodbury to John Eaton and John Coffee, October 20, 1831, John Robb to F. W. Armstrong, July 19, 1832, Eaton and Coffee to Chiefs and Headmen of the Chickasaw Nation, December 6, 1831, *Correspondence on the Subject of the Emigration of Indians,* S. Doc. 512, 2:360–61, 624, 882, 3:17; Grant Foreman, *Indian Removal: The Emigration of the Five Civilized Tribes of Indians,* new ed. (Norman: University of Oklahoma Press, 1953), 48–49.

36. Satz, "Indian Policy in the Jacksonian Era," 75, 84–88; Satz, *American Indian Policy in the Jacksonian Era,* 66, 112–15.

37. Paul W. Gates, "The Frontier Land Business in Wisconsin," *Wisconsin Magazine of History* 53 (Summer 1969): 306, 313; Nancy Oestreich Lurie, "Winnebago," in *Northeast,* ed. Trigger, 691 (fig. 1), 697–700; Robert W. Venables, "Victim Versus Victim: The Irony of the New York Indians' Removal to Wisconsin," in *American Indian Environments: Ecological Issues in Native American History,* ed. Christopher Vecsey and Robert W. Venables (Syracuse: Syracuse University Press, 1980), 140–51. For a revisionist study that argues that Jacksonian paternalism rather than land hunger was responsible for the removal of Indians from northwestern Wisconsin in 1837, see Gary C. Anderson, "The Removal of the Mdewakanton Dakota in 1837: A Case for Jacksonian Paternalism," *South Dakota History* 10 (Fall 1980): 310–33. Cf. Roy W. Meyer, *History of the Santee Sioux: United States Indian Policy on Trial* (Lincoln: University of Nebraska Press, 1967), 55–61.

38. R. David Edmunds, *The Potawatomis: Keepers of the Fire* (Norman: University of Oklahoma Press, 1978), 247–72; Howard I. McKee, "The Platte Purchase," *Missouri Historical Review* 32 (January 1938): 129–47; Spotted Tail quoted in William T. Hagan, *American Indians,* rev. ed. (Chicago: University of Chicago Press, 1979), 121. Also see n. 36, above. Elizabeth Neumeyer points out that northern Michigan provided a haven for the Indians of that state because "few farmers wanted land" there. "Michigan Indians Battle Against Removal," *Michigan History* 55 (Winter 1971): 278, 287–88.

39. See *Statutes at Large* 4:729–35; Prucha, *American Indian Policy in the Formative Years,* 250–77; Satz, *American Indian Policy in the Jacksonian Era,* 140–45, 211–36.

40. Satz, *American Indian Policy in the Jacksonian Era,* 144–45. For a case study of this phenomenon, see Thomas G. Conway, "Potawatomi Politics," *Journal of the Illinois State Historical Society* 65 (Winter 1972): 395–418. P. Richard Metcalf reminds us that tribal politics was "by no means simple, and by no means solely created or determined by whites." Borrowing Carl Becker's famous phrase, he asserts that

"the confrontation between Indians and whites was for the Indian always . . . as much a struggle over who should rule at home as over home rule." "Who Should Rule at Home? Native American Politics and Indian-White Relations," *Journal of American History* 61 (December 1974): 661, 665.

41. Berkhofer, *White Man's Indian,* 149–53; Satz, *American Indian Policy in the Jacksonian Era,* 246–78. For a comparison of the salient characteristics of the concepts of acculturation and assimilation, see Raymond H. C. Teske, Jr., and Bardin H. Nelson, "Acculturation and Assimilation: A Clarification," *American Ethnologist* 1 (May 1974): 351–67.

42. *Compilation of Messages* 3:294.

43. *Report on Memorial of American Indian Mission Association,* June 22, 1846, 29th Cong., 1st sess., H. Report 751, 1–6; *House Journal,* 29th Cong., 1st sess., 995; H.R. 490, *Original Bills,* 29th Cong., 1st sess., Library of Congress, Washington, D.C.; Satz, *American Indian Policy in the Jacksonian Era,* 211–36, 278, 294. Historian Robert F. Berkhofer, Jr., maintains that "books upon any phase of American Indian history usually contain, explicitly or implicitly, a denunciation of American policy and express sympathy for the maltreated aborigine whose culture, if not life, was destroyed. Modern scholars find a delicious irony in the disparity between classic American ideals and the actual treatment of the first Americans. Yet in terms of recent cultural theory, an even greater irony is the failure of these writers to see that earlier Americans acted as they did for the same reason that the Indians reacted as they did. Both groups behaved according to their own cultural systems. Any contradiction that the scholar finds between professed ideals and actual behavior is more a reflection of the ambivalence in past cultural assumptions than deliberate hypocrisy, unless proved otherwise, and even then the incongruity may be explained by reference to conflicting values. Thus current indictments of past American conduct are on the same plane as earlier American condemnations of savage society. The Americans of the past were victims of their cultural values just as their latter-day judges are victims of today's beliefs." *Salvation and the Savage: An Analysis of Protestant Missions and American Indian Response, 1787–1862* (Lexington: University of Kentucky Press, 1965), ix.

44. Latner, *Presidency of Andrew Jackson,* 98. Cf. Rogin, *Fathers and Children,* 4, 166–67, 182–83; Douglas T. Miller, *The Birth of Modern America, 1820–1850* (New York: Pegasus, 1970), 167.

45. Satz, *American Indian Policy in the Jacksonian Era,* 178–200.

46. Ibid., 65–66, 107–9.

47. Berkhofer, *White Man's Indian,* 162; Satz, *American Indian Policy in the Jacksonian Era,* 53–56, 151–68, 178–200; Daniel Webster to Hiram Ketchum, May 12, 1838, in Charles M. Wiltse and Harold D. Moser, eds., *The Papers of Daniel Webster:*

Correspondence, vol. 4, *1835–1839* (Hanover, N.H.: University Press of New England for Dartmouth College, 1980), 298. Edward Pessen states that "individual Whigs may have been more sensitive than their Democratic counterparts but the policies of their parties were at times remarkably similar" (*Jacksonian America*, 301). For the views of a maverick Whig in 1841, see *Memoirs of John Quincy Adams*, ed Adams, 10:491–92, and Lynn Hudson Parsons, "'A Perpetual Harrow Upon my Feelings': John Quincy Adams and the American Indian," *New England Quarterly* 46 (September 1973): 339–79.

48. Henry R. Schoolcraft, *Personal Memoirs of a Residence of Thirty Years with the Indian Tribes on the American Frontiers* (Philadelphia: Lippincott, Grambo, 1851), 318–19.

49. For the idea of Jackson as the symbol for this era, see Ward, *Andrew Jackson*.

50. Henry E. Fritz, *The Movement for Indian Assimilation, 1860–1890* (Philadelphia: University of Pennsylvania Press, 1963), 221.

51. Berkhofer, *White Man's Indian*, 153–66; Satz, *American Indian Policy in the Jacksonian Era*, 54–56; Reginald Horsman, *Race and Manifest Destiny: The Origins of American Racial Anglo-Saxonism* (Cambridge: Harvard University Press, 1981), 43–62, 189–207. The concept of progress in antebellum America is treated in Arthur A. Ekirch, *The Idea of Progress in America, 1815–1860* (New York: Columbia University Press, 1944).

52. Frances Trollope, *Domestic Manners of the Americans*, ed. Donald Smalley (1832; reprint, New York: Vintage Books, 1960), 221–22. Also see John Emmett Burke, "Andrew Jackson as Seen by Foreigners," *Tennessee Historical Quarterly* 10 (March 1951): 34.

53. George W. Featherstonhaugh, *A Canoe Voyage Up the Minnay Sotor with an account of . . . The Gold Region in the Cherokee Country; and Sketches of Popular Manners*, 2 vols. (1847; reprint, Saint Paul: Minnesota Historical Society, 1970), 2:233–34. For information on Cherokee advances in acculturation prior to removal, see Ronald N. Satz, *Tennessee's Indian Peoples: From White Contact to Removal, 1540–1840* (Knoxville: University of Tennessee Press, 1979), 72–96, and Ronald N. Satz, "Cherokee Traditionalism, Protestant Evangelism, and the Trail of Tears," *Tennessee Historical Quarterly* 44 (Fall, Winter 1985): 285–301, 380–401.

The Conflict Within: Cherokees and Removal

THEDA PERDUE

In an 1829 letter to the Congress of the United States, Gov. George Gilmer charged the Cherokee Nation with violation of Georgia's sovereignty. He reiterated his demand that the Cherokees dissolve their republican government, submit to the laws of the state, renounce their claim to territory within Georgia's chartered boundaries, and move west of the Mississippi River. Previously, Gilmer's ultimatums had generated little support beyond neighboring states; instead, many whites, particularly in New England, applauded the Cherokees' rapid adoption of Anglo-American institutions. The governor, however, predicted a surge of sympathy for Georgia. He based his prediction not on the legitimacy of the state's position but on the presumed tyranny that prevailed within the Cherokee Nation. Gilmer contended that "the oppressive system of Government which the Cherokee chiefs (principally the educated sons of white men) are now enforcing upon the body of the Indians, must soon satisfy everyone of the necessity which will compel this state to compel an end to the assumption of authority within its territory."[1] Such a political system was a repudiation of and a challenge to the ideals expressed in the democratic rhetoric of the age. The great exponent of those ideals, President Andrew Jackson, concurred with Gilmer's assessment of the situation in the Cherokee Nation and expected the Cherokee masses, perhaps following the lead of the common man in the United States, to rebel against their oppressors. In 1830, he wrote Secretary of War John Eaton: "I have no doubt but that the common Indians, seeing that their chiefs have become wealthy by the course pursued by them, whilst the common Indians have been reduced to beggary, will soon burst their bonds of slavery, and compel their chiefs to propose terms for their removal."[2] Gilmer and Jackson, of course, cannot be depended upon for dispassionate analysis of Cherokee society. But the consistency with which they and other advocates of removal charged that the leadership of the Cherokee Nation subjugated and exploited the masses suggests that we may need to take another look at the Cherokee political system and class structure. In the process we may determine whether an elite did indeed control the nation and if opposition to this elite gave rise to the pro-removal sentiment that culminated in the Treaty of New Echota.

Historical sources for the eighteenth century indicate that, at least in this period, the Cherokee political system lacked a permanent elite that exercised coercive authority. James Adair, a trader among southeastern Indians, reported that "as the law of nature appoints no frail mortal to be a king, or ruler, over his brethren . . . , the Indians, therefore, have no such titles or persons, as emperors, or kings; nor an appellative for such, in any of their dialects. Their highest title, either in military or civil life, signifies only a *Chieftain:* they have no words to express despotic power, arbitrary kings, oppressed or obedient subjects." Furthermore, Adair noted the absence of an economic class structure among southeastern Indians, who possessed instead an "equality of condition, manners, and privileges, and constant familiarity in society."[3]

Councils, in which all participated, made decisions. In the operation of these councils, the chiefs had only an advisory role. Adair commented, "The power of their chiefs is an empty sound. They can only persuade or dissuade the people by the force of good-nature and clear reasoning. . . . Their voices, to a man, have due weight in every public affair, as it concerns their welfare alike." Gen. James Edward Oglethorpe concurred. "All the power they have is no more than to call their old Men and their Captains together, and to propound to them, without Interruption, the measures they think proper. After *they* have done speaking, all the others have liberty to give their opinions also, and they reason together till they have brought each other into some unanimous Resolution." In other words, each person had an opportunity to speak, and councils discussed an issue until a consensus began to emerge. If certain individuals on the council could not agree with the arguments and line of reasoning that seemed to be gaining acceptance, they withdrew from the political arena so they would not disrupt or hinder the arrival at consensus. No one condemned this withdrawal or attempted to compel the individuals to remain on the council, abide by the decision of the majority, and participate in the implementation of the decision. Nor did those who withdrew actively oppose a decision with which they could not agree.[4]

The same ethics that governed individuals in council applied to towns within the tribe. Each town was a distinct political unit with its own council and townhouse. According to Adair, "each town is independent of another. Their own friendly compact continues the union. An obstinate war leader will sometimes commit acts of hostility, or make peace for his own town, contrary to the good liking of the rest of the nation."[5] There are many eighteenth-century examples of individuals and towns pursuing courses of action that diverged from that of the majority. During the French and Indian War, Cherokee chiefs met with South Carolina officials in an attempt to resolve red-white differences while war parties raided the English colonial frontier; Cherokee women provided food for soldiers in the besieged Fort Loudoun; and Attakullakulla rescued John Stuart from the fate that befell most of the garrison after the fort surrendered. Similarly, during the American Revolution several Cherokees supported the rebel cause while the majority of the tribe allied with the British. And following the Revolution, the Chickamauga towns in northwestern Alabama ignored the peace treaties that the Cherokees negotiated with the United States and continued to fight until 1794, when those who could not accept a truce migrated west.

Individuals and individual towns that disagreed with an emerging consensus did not attempt to subvert the dominant group. Since no concept of the loyal opposition existed in Cherokee politics, neither did they join that group to carry out a decision. Even the Chickamaugas in their violent opposition to the United States directed their hostilities against whites rather than Indians. They were not contesting the Cherokee decision for peace; they merely were refusing to abide by the decision. And just as the Chickamaugas did not force other Cherokees to join with them in their struggle, the majority did not compel the dissenters to lay down their arms.

Nevertheless, throughout the eighteenth century, political power became progressively more centralized and authority more coercive. In his study of eighteenth-century Cherokee political organization, Frederick Gearing posited that the growing necessity of controlling the bellicose activities of young warriors led to an assumption of greater power by the chiefs.[6] The punitive expeditions of English colonists in response to frontier raids injured far more individuals than those responsible for the hostilities, so in areas where the ramifications of individual decisions and actions extended to the entire group, coercive authority began to evolve.

Economic power also came to be vested in the chiefs. European powers offered guns, ammunition, blankets, knives, hatchets, kettles, sugar, and rum to Indians in exchange for their alliance. Sometimes these gifts were individual, but most often officials entrusted the goods intended for many to a prominent warrior who could use them to enlist participants in a military expedition.[7] As a result, the war chiefs became personally wealthy and established themselves as the source of wealth for others. In addition, the presence of white traders exacerbated the growing inequality in wealth. Children of traders by Indian women inherited Cherokee tribal and clan affiliation from their mothers (because of the Cherokees' matrilineal kinship system) and prosperous businesses from their fathers. Along with the warriors, the descendants of traders began to assume preeminence in the political as well as the economic structure of Cherokee society.[8]

By the end of the eighteenth century, one individual, Little Turkey, held the title of principal chief. He presided over council meetings attended by delegates from various Cherokee towns and communicated with United States officials as the spokesman for the Cherokee people. However, the principal chief was by no means omnipotent. The council and local chiefs scrupulously monitored his actions, particularly in relations with the federal government, and in the early nineteenth century when the views of the principal chief failed to reflect the dominant opinion in the nation, other chiefs did not hesitate to depose him. This radical action came in response to Principal Chief Black Fox's inclination to accept President Thomas Jefferson's proposal that the Cherokees cede their land in the east and move west to the recently acquired Louisiana Territory, where they could live in peace beyond the corrupting influence of civilization. The Indian agent Return J. Meigs and several chiefs from the Chickamauga towns supported Black Fox, but the vast majority of Cherokees vehemently opposed the plan. A confederation of prominent chiefs removed Black Fox from office in 1808 and installed Path Killer, one of their number, as principal chief. By 1810 the crisis had passed with some Cherokees departing and others remaining, and Black Fox resumed his position as principal chief.[9]

During this same period, the Cherokees took steps to establish a more formal political system. In 1808, the council recorded the first written law, which provided for the organization of a national police force, the light-horse guard, to protect property and to ensure the inheritance rights of widows and orphans.[10] The property to which this legislation referred was not real estate but chattel property and improvements. The Cherokees held real estate in common, and a man could cultivate as much as he required as long as he did not infringe on the rights of others. The removal of Black Fox was intended to protect real property; the organization of a light-horse guard was intended to protect other forms of property.[11] Therefore, from the time of the first removal crisis, the government of the Cherokee Nation, cognizant of dangers to private and common property, dedicated itself to the protection of both.

Over the next twenty years, the Cherokees developed increasingly complex governmental machinery in order to protect these two species of property. The council, an informal body composed of chiefs from the various towns within the territory claimed by the Cherokees, voted in 1817 to establish a standing committee to manage the affairs of the nation when the general legislative council was not in session. The members of the council also unanimously adopted articles of government "in order to obviate the evil consequences" of independent towns and unauthorized individuals negotiating the concession of common land between council meetings. The document reaffirmed the right of individuals to improvements (interestingly, according to the principle of matrilineal descent) and deprived emigrants of any claim to common property.[12]

The standing committee established by the articles of government in 1817 was the first step in delegated legislative power; the second was the law enacted in 1820 that provided for the division of the Cherokee Nation into eight districts, each of which elected four representatives to the council. The council also authorized the construction of a council house in each district where disputes could be resolved and cases involving national law could be tried. In 1822, a supreme court was convened in the capital, New Echota, to hear appeals from the district courts.[13] National laws and the institutions erected to enforce and implement them gradually superseded traditional kinship groups and local town councils, which except for relatively insignificant matters became superfluous. About 1835, J. P. Evans traveled in the Cherokee Nation and commented: "Although the excellent laws & regulations which were adopted and put into practice some few years ago, by the council of the nation, through the exertions of enlightened men, were regularly executed until the seizure of the country by the States; yet the influence of the patriarchs in their respective towns was considerable; especially in matters of minor importance; wherein they presided and made decisions which the parties saw proper to obey. But in most, (an in all criminal and important), cases, the written laws triumphed over the old barbarous customs."[14]

The centralization of political power, the delegation of authority, and the usurpation of local and family responsibilities by a national government drastically reduced the number of people who participated in the decision-making process. These political changes also reduced the number of people with whom United States officials needed to deal. Some Cherokees perceived a danger in such delegated power: those who held that power might be tempted to cede tribal land for personal gain. In the past, the United States had granted personal reservations (private tracts within ceded land) to prominent Cherokees as rewards and as bribes. Usually continuing to live within the nation, the recipients held their reservations until property values increased and then sold the land at a handsome profit, which they subsequently invested in improvements on common land belonging to the nation.

Recognition of the risks involved in concentrating political power in the hands of a few contributed to the growing dissatisfaction with the national government among many Cherokee traditionalists. The first manifestation of discontent came in 1824 when the chiefs of Etowah (Hightower) asked that missionaries be withdrawn from their town because the minister prohibited converts from meeting in the council house. This restriction prevented Christians from participating in local government and forced them to look to the district and national governments for redress of grievances.[15] By 1826, mere dissatisfaction had turned to open opposition to the national government. A member of the council, White Path, was expelled by his colleagues for subversive activities and was replaced by the brother of the assistant principal chief.[16] When the council voted to call a convention of delegates from the eight districts to meet in the summer of 1827 and draft a constitution for the nation, rebellion threatened. Samuel A. Worcester, a missionary of the American Board of Commissioners for Foreign Missions, wrote the society's Boston headquarters in March. "A dissatisfied party have held a Council, at which they are said to have had some from every district in the Nation, except one, (not, however, *chiefs* from all,) and took it upon them to say what should be and what should not be in regard to the affairs of Government and to repeal and enact laws. They however took no measures to secure the execution of their laws, yet for want of a system, and of energetic leaders, I presume the faction is not much to be dreaded." The traditionalists held all-night dances and employed conjury, and as the time appointed for the convention approached, the missionaries became more apprehensive. Isaac Proctor reported that the opposition party was "much the largest," and William Chamberlain warned of a "grand and united effort to destroy the government and drive religion and all improvement from the Nation."[17]

United States agents as well as missionaries were aware of the traditionalists' reaction to republicanism. John Cocke, a commissioner appointed to negotiate a Cherokee removal treaty, notified the secretary of war in 1827 of his intention to attend the impending conclave. "The object of the Council or convention is understood to be the formulation of a written constitution. I believe considerable excitement now exists among the Indians as to what policy shall be pursued. The mixed bloods are known to have been for some time at the head of affairs and passed laws so contrary to ancient customs that the native Indian is ready to revolt." While he was in New Echota, Cocke received a number of Indian visitors, including the clerk of the council, Elias Boudinot. Boudinot told the federal official and his entourage that a previous meeting of the council had adjourned because "some of the old Indians were much dissatisfied and intended to raise their opposition to their new mode of government by a Constitution."[18] Cocke's report of the constitutional convention probably provided some basis for Gilmer and Jackson's belief that the Cherokee chiefs were oppressing the "common Indians."

The participants in White Path's rebellion, as the opposition to the constitution of 1827 came to be known, were certainly "common Indians." Living at the subsistence level, most cultivated farms of fewer than ten acres and produced only enough to satisfy their families' needs. Their improvements generally were limited to a one- or two-room log house and perhaps a few fruit trees. American Board missionaries reported that the opponents of the constitution had only one "considerable man among them of reputable character," probably meaning a member of their congregation, and that even he was decidedly "lower class."[19] Apparently, few of the rebels could be considered prominent in the political or economic life of the nation.

The followers of White Path rarely had participated in Cherokee politics on the national level because in the first two decades of the nineteenth century political power had become further concentrated in the hands of an elite. When the Mohawk Maj. John Norton visited the Cherokees in 1809, he observed that a relatively small group had assumed authority on the basis of "real or imaginary talents" or "because they have wealth." The delegates to the constitutional convention clearly were members of an economic as well as a political elite. The twelve signers of the constitution who can be located on the Henderson Roll of 1835 owned 355 slaves, approximately 23 percent of all those in the Cherokee Nation, and at least seven of the signers had received previous reservations from the United States. The twelve farmed an acreage four times the average for Cherokee heads of households and produced five times as much corn and six times as much wheat as other Cherokees.[20]

Among the Cherokee founding fathers were such entrepreneurs as John and Lewis Ross, John Martin, and Joseph Vann. John and Lewis Ross had received private reservations in Tennessee in 1819 and subsequently had purchased additional acreage outside the Cherokee Nation for speculation. The brothers retained their Cherokee citizenship, however, and continued to reside in the nation. One plantation belonging to John Ross, principal chief and president of the constitutional convention, was at the head of the Coosa River within the territory claimed by Georgia. He lived there in a two-story weatherboarded house with four fireplaces and twenty glass windows. Outbuildings included workshops, smokehouses, stables, corn-cribs, a blacksmith shop, a wagon house, and quarters for his 19 slaves. John Ross also owned peach and apple orchards and operated a profit-able ferry on the Coosa River.[21] Lewis Ross, one of the major Cherokee merchants, had two or three large stores in the nation, a mill, and three ferryboats. Master of more than forty slaves, he lived in what visiting New Englanders described as "an elegant white house near the bank of the river, as neatly furnished as almost any in Litchfield County [and] Negroes enough to wait on us."[22] Lewis Ross occupied various offices in the nation, including president of the standing committee and district marshall. John Martin, chief justice of the Cherokee Supreme Court and later treasurer of the nation, owned 69 slaves, who raised six thousand bushels of corn in 1835. Also a reservee, Martin could afford to maintain separate households for his two wives.[23] Perhaps the wealthiest man in the Cherokee Nation, Joseph Vann lived in the magnificent red-brick mansion that his father had built at Springplace in northern Georgia. In 1835, he owned 110 slaves, who cultivated 300 acres, and operated a mill, a ferry, and a tavern.[24]

Clearly, these men were not "common Indians." Their wealth set them apart from their constituents (as well as from most Georgians, who coveted Cherokee land). The Rosses, Martin, Vann, and others among the governing elite had received a formal education and had inherited money, slaves, businesses, houses, and other improvements. They combined their training and perhaps talent and ambition with capital, and parlayed their legacies into even greater fortunes. Such men formed a Cherokee aristocracy, and their values as well as their means separated them from the "common Indians" who supported White Path.

At the constitutional convention of 1827, the Cherokee aristocracy managed to appease the followers of White Path. Whether compromise or coercion produced agreement is unknown, but probably the elite and the "common Indians" realized that divisiveness threatened the homeland that the latter valued and the improvement on which the former's economic status depended. The document drafted by the convention pledged that the new government would protect the common title to the land as well as individual titles to improvements. The first article defined the limits of the Cherokee Nation, declared that those boundaries "shall hereafter remain unalterably the same," guaranteed that "the lands herein are, and shall remain, the common property of the Nation," and reaffirmed that individuals owned the improvements that they made on common property as long as they remained citizens of the nation.[25] The resolute commitment of the new government to the protection of common and private property no doubt helped reconcile the "common Indians" and the elite, and subsequent legislation that prohibited active opposition quieted the irreconcilable.

The constitution represented a victory for republicanism. The government that it established had executive, legislative, and judicial branches. The bicameral legislature consisted of the committee and the council, to which districts elected two and three members respectively. Therefore, despite White Path's rebellion, centralized and delegated political power remained a feature of Cherokee political organization, and many of those who had written the constitution were elected to the offices it created.

The new constitution continued several practices that favored the Cherokee elite. The document permitted the council to require a bond from certain officials. In some cases, the bond effectively prevented anyone who was not wealthy from holding that office. For example, law required the national marshal to post a bond of $5,000 and the national treasurer to present ten securities totaling $50,000. Even district marshals had to post bond of $1,000.[26] Consequently, members of the elite monopolized certain offices, particularly those involving finance and enforcement.

Under the constitution, the national council retained the right to regulate aspects of the economy. In practice, the council sometimes delegated the administration of regulatory legislation to other officials such as the national treasurer or the marshals, but the privilege of regulation remained firmly vested in the council. In particular, the national government gave individuals and associations the right to operate toll roads and ferries and prohibited competition. Although rates were fixed by the government, which ultimately exempted citizens from turnpike charges, the volume of travel was sufficient to make toll roads and ferries extremely lucrative enterprises.[27] For example, the ferry valued at $10,000 that John Ross operated on the Coosa River brought in approximately $1,000 annually.[28] In addition to turnpikes and ferries, the national supervision of transportation extended to public roads. The council awarded contracts for maintenance of segments of the federal road to the lowest bidders. Until 1828, the maintenance contracts were divided into ten shares, but in that year the council reduced the number of shares to eight. The law required contractors to give bond for the performance of their duties, and the corresponding increase in the amount of the bond for each contract probably excluded some people from competitive bidding.[29]

The national government continued to grant permits and licenses under the new constitution. The original licensing law of 1819 required citizens who operated stores or sold sugar, coffee, salt, iron, and steel to purchase licenses for $25. Until the fee was lowered to $12 in 1822 and then suspended in 1829, the system limited merchandising to those who had not only enough capital to set up shop but also enough cash to purchase a license.[30] Furthermore, the acceptance or rejection of a license application was the prerogative of national officials.

Another government prerogative was the issuance of permits to Cherokees who wished to hire whites. In 1819, the council passed a law that required permits for the employment of whites as "schoolmasters, blacksmiths, millers, salt petre and gun powder manufacturers, ferrymen, and turnpike keepers, and mechanics." After 1828, the council taxed employers $1 for each permit.[31] While the system had neither an exclusionary intent nor effect, the council issued permits solely at its discretion.

In some ways, the Cherokee government functioned as a national bank. In 1825, the council authorized the treasurer to make loans to Cherokee citizens who "may be fully able to repay the sum or sums loaned, and also shall give bond and two good and sufficient securities." The legislation limited the amount of the loan to $500 and the duration to six months (with the possibility of renewal upon payment of interest) and specified the interest rate to be 6 percent. In order to borrow money, however, one had to own property (that is, improvements) equal in value to the loan.[32]

The government also had a hand in private financial transactions. The council established a lawful interest ceiling of 6 percent and passed legislation that protected contracts and facilitated the collection of debts. Marshals sold at public auction the belongings of those who defaulted on money debts, seized improvements, chattels, and produce (except for sixty bushels of corn) for the satisfaction of property bonds, and attached the possessions of anyone suspected of planning to leave the nation without paying his creditors.[33] The national newspaper, the *Cherokee Phoenix,* published advertisements of bankruptcy sales, repudiations of notes, and bond redemptions,[34] and one-third of the cases heard by the Cherokee Supreme Court involved debt.[35] The names of national officials appeared in both the *Phoenix* and the supreme court docket, usually as creditors.

The national government's preoccupation with commerce and finance does not mean that the leaders were callous toward the economic needs and difficulties of the "common Indians." Indeed, several measures indicate a strong paternalistic sentiment on the part of the aristocracy. For example, the national government purchased the improvements of traditionalists who lived within the bounds of New Echota when town lots in the new capital were surveyed and offered for sale. The council refused to do the same for two of its members and required them to purchase the lots containing their improvements at prevailing prices. In another example of official paternalism, the council appropriated funds for the care of Big Bear, an old blind man who had no family to nurse him.[36] But in general, the aristocracy primarily was concerned with increasing and protecting its wealth, to which the "common Indians" did not object so long as they were not exploited directly. When it came to opposing efforts by the United States, Georgia, Tennessee, and Alabama to force the nation west of the Mississippi, the common Indians gave the aristocracy their wholehearted support.

The political realignment of 1827 placed John Ross and White Path on the same side and pitted them against a major internal challenge to the privileges of the elite and the will of the masses. This challenge came from a group of men who aspired to the aristocracy but lacked either the financial base, the political power, or the family connections to gain entry. Perhaps we can call these men a "rising middle class," although agriculture rather than commerce provided their livelihood. Certainly their values, which centered on materialism, acquisitiveness, and individualism, separated them from the masses, and their means denied most of them access to the elite. In this sense, as well as in others, they were in the middle. This rising middle class, envious of the wealth and power of the elite and disdainful of the desires of the masses, saw in the removal issue an opportunity to usurp political authority and to reap rewards and concessions from the United States. Members of this class, and not the "common Indians," are the ones who ultimately "burst their bonds of slavery" by negotiating a removal treaty.

As early as 1830, the United States government identified the resentful middle class as the Cherokee faction most likely to negotiate a removal treaty. In order to encourage cooperation, officials contemplated using the same tactic that already had proved successful—the granting of reservations in fee simple to those who would agree to a land cession. Most members of the Cherokee middle class previously had not received reservations, and they apparently were jealous of the economic advantage that reservations had given the aristocracy. In 1830, United States Commissioner John Lowrey concluded his report on treaty discussions:

> I must beg leave to add, that notwithstanding that they have at present refused to accede to any propositions that have been made them, yet in my humble opinion, a revolutionary work is at this time fast progressing amongst them; a goodly number of them now want reservations, and those are men of influence. They say that many of their chiefs and counsellors have heretofore had the benefit of reservations; that they have become rich, and built elegant houses, and purchased splendid furniture, and in whose hands are now placed all the good offices of the nation, and are in reality the rulers of the country; while others, equally worthy, have not participated in such bounties.

The Cherokee Council adamantly refused personal reservations in exchange for a removal treaty: "We have no disposition to alter the extent of our reservation, as defined by former treaties—the limits of the whole Cherokee Nation."[37] Georgia also objected to reservations, so United States commissioners decided instead to concentrate on obtaining cession of the territory and removal of the entire nation to the West.

United States officials discovered another complaint of those who were disposed to negotiate: many were deeply in debt to such members of the aristocracy as Lewis Ross and Joseph Vann. The enrolling agent Benjamin Currey wrote the secretary of war in 1831. "Most of those inclined to go to the west are indebted to the rich and powerful chiefs, many of whom are opposed to the emigration policy, and would throw any obstacle in the way, short of open hostilities, to thwart the views of the government on the subject; whilst those disposed to go, but not having the means to satisfy the demands of their creditors, intimidated by the terrors of the law, would, in most cases, perhaps, abandon all idea of immigration, and become vassals again to the more powerful chiefs." The War Department authorized the payment of debts, not to exceed the value of improvements, for those who would enroll, but the funds appropriated fell short of the amount required. Currey complained that $10,000 dollars was "not sufficient by one half, to answer the demands that will be made. Those who enrolled under these pledges are of the wealthiest unconnected with the Indian government."[38]

The middle class found President Jackson and most members of his administration to be sympathetic to its plight. In part, this was because members of the middle class were almost the only Cherokees interested in moving. But perhaps equally important was the analogy that Jackson made between Cherokee society and his own, and he saw in the Cherokee middle class people similar to those who had elected him. Furthermore, their complaints against the aristocracy resembled his own objections to the privileged elite in the United States. Jackson's pronouncements on Indian removal closely follow his campaign rhetoric in 1828: one simply substitutes John Ross for John Adams, the Cherokee aristocracy for the supporters of Adams, and the treaty party for the Democrats. Thus Jackson equated the struggle within Cherokee society to the conflict that he perceived in his own society between an energetic middle class and a corrupt upper class. He sought to help the Cherokee middle class win its struggle as he had the white middle class, and instead of the demise of the national bank, the symbol for victory became a removal treaty. The steadfast opposition of Ross, Martin, and Vann to a removal treaty confirmed Jackson's belief that removal was best for the "common Indian."

Several obstacles to securing a removal treaty for the "common Indians" stood in Jackson's way. Since Georgia laws made it impossible to hold elections for national officials after 1830, no chance existed for replacing these men constitutionally with more pliable ones. Furthermore, the electorate actually showed little desire for a change in leadership and attempted to maintain the semblance of republicanism by meeting in council in Tennessee to ratify emergency political measures. At the same time, the national government took steps to silence dissent. The columns of the *Phoenix* were closed to debate on the removal issue. When the editor became a proponent of negotiation, he was removed from his position, and three members of the national council were impeached for favoring removal.[39] The aristocracy, in adopting these repressive tactics, sought to save itself as well as the Cherokee Nation. And the only outcry among the Cherokees came from the small, dissatisfied, and ambitious middle class who eventually negotiated removal.

In 1832, a pro-treaty party began to coalesce around the leadership of Major Ridge, his son John Ridge, and the deposed editor, Elias Boudinot. The elite, who controlled the government, continued to refuse to negotiate a removal treaty, so United States officials turned to the unauthorized treaty party. In December 1835, they signed the Treaty of New Echota, by which the Cherokee Nation relinquished its land in the East and agreed to move west of the Mississippi River. Most of those who signed the treaty were not members of the "elite," nor were they really "common Indians." Eleven of the twenty-five for whom data are available owned slaves, while only 8 percent of other heads of households in the Cherokee Nation were slaveholders. Nevertheless, the total number of slaves held by treaty party members was merely one hundred, less than 7 percent of the total number of slaves in the Cherokee Nation, and only three signers listed more than ten slaves on the removal roll: Major Ridge had fifteen, John Ridge twenty-one, and John Gunter thirty. Signers of the treaty averaged 100 acres in cultivation and corn production of 1,229 bushels, as compared to only 18 acres and 219 bushels of corn for the nation as a whole. Almost two-thirds of the signers marketed corn, and in general, their prosperity seems to have rested on agriculture rather than commerce.[40]

Although members of the treaty party were better off economically than the vast majority of Cherokees, they found some avenues to wealth blocked by the aristocracy in the government. Only two signers were reservees, and the council's refusal to permit the opening of a reservation office denied others the opportunity to profit through land speculation. Published legislation indicates that none operated a turnpike, and only Major Ridge had been given permission to run a ferry. Furthermore, several of the signers' names appeared frequently in the *Phoenix* or on the court docket as debtors, so legislation in the interest of creditors affected them adversely.

Part of these men's economic problems resulted from their being political outsiders. None of the treaty signers served in the constitutional convention of 1827, and only Major Ridge and John Ridge held elective offices (although others occupied appointive positions: Andrew Ross was a judge, Stand Watie was a clerk, and Elias Boudinot was an editor). Some did not stand outside the halls of power by choice. Five men who became identified with the treaty party (James Starr, Andrew Ross, David Vann, Elias Boudinot, and John Walker, Jr.) met defeat in the election for delegates to the constitutional convention, and four of the unsuccessful candidates for the committee in 1828 (John Ridge, Major Ridge, Tesataesky, and James Foster) attached their signatures to the removal treaty. Many of the losers envisioned an aristocratic conspiracy to keep them from power, and John Ridge believed that only the ban on elections prevented his accession as principal chief.[41]

Negotiations with the United States catapulted the treaty party into the political limelight. Flattered by United States recognition as chiefs, the treaty party began to depict its members as "men of intelligence and patriotism" interested only in saving the Cherokee Nation from "political thraldom and moral degradation." Elias Boudinot, perhaps the most articulate advocate of a removal treaty, pointed out that "what is termed the 'Cherokee question' may be considered in two points of view: the controversy with the States and the General Government, and the controversy among the Cherokees themselves." And within this internal controversy, the treaty party insisted that its only concern was for the masses, who were "so completely blinded as not to see the destruction which awaits them."[42]

In reality, self-interest was the primary motivation for most members of the treaty party, and their rewards were not long in coming. Gov. Wilson Lumpkin of Georgia offered protection for the property of those Cherokees who seemed to be disposed to negotiate. In 1834, he instructed the federal enrolling officer to "assure Boudinot, Ridge, and their friends of state protection under any circumstances. I shall feel it my imperative duty to pay due regard to the situation and afford them every security which our laws will justify or authorize." The lots on which those favoring removal had improvements were temporarily withdrawn from the lottery or declared exempt from immediate confiscation.[43] While opponents of removal such as John Ross and Joseph Vann were unceremoniously evicted by the Georgians who had drawn their holdings in the state's land lottery, treaty party members continued to live in their homes and profit from their improvements. Furthermore, the Treaty of New Echota provided preemption rights for those Cherokees judged capable of managing their affairs under state law.[44] Although the supplemental articles attached to the treaty in the spring of 1836 voided this provision, the signers of the treaty, who made up at least half of the committee that was to decide on preemptions, originally intended to make it possible for themselves and other highly acculturated Cherokees to avoid the consequences of their actions.

Members of the treaty party were equally disappointed in their desire to achieve political power within the Cherokee Nation through negotiations with the United States government. Jackson did not stand for reelection in 1836, and the succeeding Van Buren administration reluctantly acknowledged the popularity of John Ross. Believing that the principal chief's cooperation was essential to effecting Cherokee removal, the federal government opened negotiations with Ross and, subsequently, agreed to raise the amount of money paid the Cherokees under the terms of the Treaty of New Echota and to permit them to conduct their own removal. The agreement with Ross meant that the Cherokee government controlled lucrative contracts for supplying the migrants, and the contracts went not to members of the treaty party but to Lewis Ross.[45] In the end, therefore, members of the treaty party did not retain federal recognition as "chiefs"; they only forced the real chiefs into negotiating (and profiting from) removal.

Immediately after removal, ploys to catapult the treaty party into power failed. Although members of the treaty party joined forces with the Old Settlers, those Cherokees who had removed before the Treaty of New Echota, John Ross still commanded the allegiance of the majority. Perhaps more significant, the executions of Major Ridge, John Ridge, and Elias Boudinot, the most highly regarded of the conspirators, deprived the treaty party of the kind of leadership that could have made it a more credible force in Indian-white relations. Finally, the civil war that raged until 1846 was economically disruptive to all parties and alienated many Old Settlers who originally had been sympathetic to the treaty party. The truce arranged in 1846 between Ross and Stand Watie, brother of Boudinot, firmly established Ross as the principal chief of a united Cherokee Nation.

A remnant of the treaty party, led by Watie, tried once again to unseat

Ross in the American Civil War by allying with the Confederacy. But it was not until after the war and Ross's death in 1866 that the class that had supported removal began to gain ascendancy. Even then, these ambitious men did not ride to victory on a groundswell of popular support. Instead, they followed the lead of Boudinot's son, Elias Cornelius Boudinot, and accepted employment and shares of stock from railroad, mining, and timber companies. These biological and philosophical descendants of the treaty party circumvented tribal legislation intended to restrict the outside investment of capital and actively promoted corporate expansion in Indian territory.[46] They rejoiced in the ultimate outcome of this expansion—a rapid influx of whites, allotment of Indian land to individuals, distribution of "excess" land, dissolution of the Cherokee government, and admission to the state of Oklahoma, in which Indians were a minority.

This sequence of events was, in some ways, the culmination of the conflict that began in the old Cherokee Nation in the East. A wealthy and powerful elite had tried to protect itself by restraining the ambition and greed of other Cherokees. In the process, the elite won the support of the masses, who did not share its materialistic values, and the enmity of a rising middle class whose acquisitiveness the elite thwarted. The removal issue seemed to provide an opportunity for this small middle class to subvert the elite, but the masses refused to rally to the removal cause. Outsiders, including the governor of Georgia and the president of the United States, attributed the Cherokees' refusal to migrate to the power of the elite. Actually, the only Indians who found the Cherokee leaders despotic were the relatively few who wished to join or displace them. The inability of this class to achieve its political and economic goals, rather than strong pro-removal sentiments, led them to negotiate Cherokee removal.

NOTES

1. *Correspondence on the Subject of the Emigration of Indians,* 23d Cong., 1st sess., S. Doc. 512, 2:223.

2. Ibid., 186–87.

3. James Adair, *History of the American Indians,* ed. Samuel Cole Williams (1775; reprint, Watauga Press, Johnson City, Tenn.: 1930), 406–7, 459–60.

4. Ibid., 460; *Gentleman's Magazine* 3 (August 1733): 414.

5. Adair, *History of the American Indians,* ed. Williams, 460.

6. Frederick O. Gearing, *Priests and Warriors: Social Structures for Cherokee Politics in the Eighteenth Century* (Menasha, Wis.: American Anthropological Association, 1962).

7. William L. McDowell, ed., *Journals of the Commissioners of the Indian Trade, Sept. 20, 1710–Aug. 29, 1718* (Columbia, S.C.: South Carolina Archives Department, 1955).

8. Emmet Starr, *History of the Cherokee Indians* (Oklahoma City: Warden, 1921), 303–476.

9. William G. McLoughlin, "Thomas Jefferson and the Beginning of Cherokee Nationalism," *William and Mary Quarterly,* 3d ser., 32 (1975): 547–80.

10. *Laws of the Cherokee Nation: Adopted by the Council at Various Times, Reprinted for the Benefit of the Nation* (Tahlequah, Cherokee Nation, 1852), 3–4.

11. John P. Reid, *A Law of Blood: The Primitive Law of the Cherokee Nation* (New York: New York University Press, 1970), 123–42.

12. *Laws,* 4–5.

13. Ibid., 11–12, 28.

14. J. P. Evans, "Sketches of Cherokee Characteristics," *Journal of Cherokee Studies* 4 (1979): 10–20.

15. McLoughlin, "Cherokee Anti-Mission Sentiment, 1824–1828," *Ethnohistory* 21 (1974): 361–70.

16. *Laws,* 66–67.

17. Samuel A. Worcester to Jeremiah Evarts, March 29, 1827, Isaac Proctor to Evarts, May 10, 1827, William Chamberlain to Evarts, May 3, 1827, Records of the American Board of Commissioners for Foreign Missions, Houghton Library, Harvard University, Cambridge, Mass.

18. John Cocke to Secretary of War, July 1, 1827, Journal of the Commissioners, July 3, 1827, Office of Indian Affairs, Letters Received, 1824–81, Record Group 75, National Archives, Washington, D.C.

19. Worcester to Evarts, March 19, 1827, Report on the Station at Haweis, January 1828, Records of the American Board.

20. Carl F. Klinck and James J. Talman, eds., *The Journal of Major John Norton, 1816* (Toronto: Publications of the Champlain Society, 1970), 135; Cherokee Census of 1835 (Henderson Roll), Record Group 75, National Archives.

21. Gary E. Moulton, *John Ross: Cherokee Chief* (Athens: University of Georgia Press, 1978), 20, 30–31.

22. Census of 1835; Benjamin Gold to Hezekiah Gold, December 8, 1829, Cherokee Letters Collection, Georgia Department of Archives, Atlanta, Ga.

23. Census of 1835; James F. Corn, *Red Clay and Rattlesnake Springs* (Cleveland, Tenn.: Walsworth, 1976), 48–51.

24. Census of 1835; Clemens de Baillou, "The Chief Vann House, the Vann's Tavern and Ferry," *Early Georgia* 2 (1957): 3–11. Another founding father and member of the Cherokee elite was Edward Gunter, who operated two ferryboats, owned about 30 slaves, and cultivated 235 acres producing 4,000 bushels of corn in 1835. Gunter also served as a member of the constitutional conventions of 1827 and 1839 and was a signer of the constitutions produced. Gunter was also a member of the executive council in 1834 and signed the Act of Union in 1839.

25. *Laws*, 118–30.

26. Ibid., 58, 67, 91.

27. Ibid., 7–8, 13, 20–23.

28. Moulton, *John Ross*, 31.

29. *Laws*, 35, 138.

30. Ibid., 5–6, 30, 139.

31. Ibid., 6, 99.

32. Ibid., 50.

33. Ibid., 113.

34. *Cherokee Phoenix*, February 21, March 6, November 12, 1828, May 27, July 1, November 4, 11, 1829, October 8, 1830, May 7, 1831, May 19, November 18, 1832.

35. Cherokee Supreme Court Docket, Cherokee Collection, Tennessee State Library and Archives, Nashville, Tenn.

36. *Laws*, 63–64, 145.

37. S. Doc. 512, 2:178–80.

38. Ibid., 376, 385–86, 612–15, 676–77.

39. Elias Boudinot, *Documents in Relation to the Validity of the Cherokee Treaty of 1835*, 25th Cong., 2d sess., S. Doc. 121, 5.

40. Census of 1835.

41. *Cherokee Phoenix*, May 14, August 13, 1828; *Laws*, 73–76, 130.

42. S. Doc. 121, 1–2, 10.

43. Georgia Governor's Letterbook, 1833, Georgia Department of Archives, Atlanta, Ga.

44. Charles J. Kappler, comp. and ed., *Indian Affairs: Laws and Treaties*, 5 vols. (Washington, D.C.: Government Printing Office, 1904–41), 2:439–49.

45. Gary E. Moulton, "Chief John Ross and Cherokee Removal Finances," *Chronicles of Oklahoma* 52 (1974): 342–59.

46. For an excellent study of this period, see H. Craig Miner, *The Corporation and the Indian: Tribal Sovereignty and Industrial Civilization in Indian Territory, 1865–1907* (Columbia: University of Missouri Press, 1976).

The Demography of the Trail of Tears Period: A New Estimate of Cherokee Population Losses

RUSSELL THORNTON

I t is estimated that as many as 100,000 American Indians were removed from eastern homelands to west of the Mississippi River during the first half of the nineteenth century (Blue 1974, iii; Doran 1975–76, 496–97); this may even be an underestimation. Most of the total number were members of five tribes: Cherokee, Chickasaw, Choctaw, Creek, and Seminole, along with remnants of other southeastern Indian groups. Most relocations occurred in the decade following passage of the United States Indian Removal Act of 1830 (Prucha 1975, 52–53), though some occurred earlier and some later.

BACKGROUND TO REMOVAL

During the seventeenth and eighteenth centuries, particularly the latter, the seeds of a massive nineteenth-century removal of American Indians to reservation lands by the United States government were sown. This took the form of seventeenth-century colonial governments restricting eastern American Indians to particular areas, sometimes involving localized relocations of American Indians. The governments established, for example, both "praying towns" for Christianized Indians in New England

and various state "reservations," for example, the Mashpee Reservation on Cape Cod (1660), the Poosepatuck Reservation on Long Island (1666), the Pequot Reservation in Connecticut (1683), the Fall River Reservation in Massachusetts (1709), and the Gay Head Reservation on Martha's Vineyard (1711). Also, some American Indians were persuaded to leave former tribal lands for new ones to the west. The Stockbridge, for instance, had moved to New York from Massachusetts by 1789 (and then moved to present-day Wisconsin in the early 1800s).

This was the precedent of a massive removal and relocation of American Indian tribes that would occur in the nineteenth century. Further groundwork was laid in the eighteenth century when the United States War Department was established in August 1789, because Indian removal and relocation would eventually be a function of the department (Prucha 1975, 14). On March 11, 1824, the Bureau of Indian Affairs was created within the War Department (Prucha 1975, 37–38), and it remained there until the Department of the Interior was established in 1849 (Prucha 1975, 80).

On May 28, 1830, Congress passed the Indian Removal Act. The act provided for the exchange of American Indian lands in any state or territory of the United States, but especially in the southern United States, for lands west of the Mississippi River and, additionally, for the removal of American Indians to them. In part, it read:

> *Be it enacted* . . . , That it shall and may be lawful for the President of the United States to cause so much of any territory belonging to the United States, west of the river Mississippi, not included in any state or organized territory, and to which the Indian title has been extinguished, as he may judge necessary, to be divided into a suitable number of districts, for the reception of such tribes or nations of Indians as may choose to exchange the lands where they now reside, and remove there; and to cause each of said districts to be so described by natural or artificial marks, as to be easily distinguished from every other. . . .

> *Sec. 2. And be it further enacted,* That it shall and may be lawful for the President to exchange any or all of such districts, so to be laid off and described, with any tribe or nation of Indians now residing within the limits of any of the states or territories, and with which the United States have existing treaties, for the whole or any part or portion of the terri-

tory claimed and occupied by such tribe or nation, within the bounds of any one or more of the states or territories, where the land claimed and occupied by the Indians, is owned by the United States, or the United States are bound to the state within which it lies to extinguish the Indian claim thereto. (Prucha 1975, 52–53)

The act was effectively used by President Andrew Jackson to remove southern tribes and relocate them on lands west of the Mississippi River, thereby securing Indian lands east of the river for settlement by the expanding non-Indian populations of the United States.

Removals and relocations always, it seems, resulted in tragedies, including population losses, for the American Indians involved. Exceptionally tragic was the removal of the Cherokees from the Southeast to Indian Territory during the late 1830s. It was such an ordeal that Cherokees subsequently named the journey *Nunna daul Isunyi*, literally, the Trail Where We Cried; it has become known in English as the Trail of Tears. The Cherokees suffered from weather, soldiers, inadequate food, disease, bereavement, and loss of homes, all of which caused large population losses. How large the losses were is the topic of this essay.

CHEROKEE POPULATION HISTORY TO 1835

Aboriginal Cherokee population size can only be conjectured because little is known of pre-European Cherokee history. Part of the conjecture concerns the identity of pre-European Cherokees and the likelihood of unrecorded epidemics of European disease prior to direct and extensive European contact with the Cherokees. It has been estimated, however, that there were more than 22,000 Cherokees during the 1600s (Mooney 1928, 8). Probably the Cherokee numbered somewhat more at an earlier date. As I have indicated elsewhere (Thornton in press), aboriginal Cherokee population size may have reached 30,000. What is certain, however, is that following direct, extensive European contact, the Cherokees suffered depopulations from disease and warfare, and their numbers declined markedly. By the early nineteenth century, the Cherokee numbered only somewhat more than 13,000 (McLoughlin and Conser 1977, 702; Thornton forthcoming). Their population increased during the next few decades;

by 1835 they numbered about what they had in the 1600s—some 22,000 (McLoughlin and Conser 1977, 702; Thornton in press).

CHEROKEE REMOVAL

Although Cherokee lands had once been immense, their exact boundaries are not known; lands the Cherokee claimed at one time or another extended from the Ohio River south almost to present-day Atlanta, Georgia, and west from present-day Virginia, North Carolina, and South Carolina across present-day Tennessee, Kentucky, and Alabama, toward the Illinois River. By the close of the revolutionary war, Cherokee tribal lands had shrunk considerably in the north and east as populations of Euro-Americans settled these areas. By the mid-1830s, Cherokee Country—as it was called—encompassed only the area where North Carolina, Tennessee, Georgia, and Alabama more or less converge.

Eventually a treaty between the Cherokees and the United States government was signed, but not by the principal officers of the Cherokee Nation. Known as the Treaty of New Echota, Georgia, where the Cherokee capital was located (having moved to the west from Echota), the Cherokee ceded to the United States their lands in the Southeast in exchange for lands in Indian Territory and $15 million. Leaders of the Cherokee Nation, under Chief John Ross, protested violently during the ensuing years. The protests were to no avail; the treaty was eventually consummated.

In the meantime, some Cherokees had voluntarily moved west. Most, however, remained in their homelands, still not believing they would be forced to leave. In 1838 the Cherokees were disarmed, and Gen. Winfield Scott was sent to oversee their removal. James Mooney describes what happened.

The history of this Cherokee removal of 1838, as gleaned by the author from the lips of actors in the tragedy, may well exceed in weight of grief and pathos any other passage in American history. Even the much-sung exile of the Acadians falls far behind it in its sum of death and misery. Under Scott's orders the troops were disposed at various points throughout the Cherokee country, where stockade forts were erected for gathering in and holding the Indians preparatory to removal. From these, squads of troops were sent to search out with rifle and bayonet every small cabin hidden away in the coves or by the sides of mountain streams, to seize and bring in as prisoners all the occupants, however or wherever they might be found. Families at dinner were startled by the sudden gleam of bayonets in the doorway and rose up to be driven with blows and oaths along the weary miles of trail that led to the stockade. Men were seized in their fields or going along the road, women were taken from their wheels and children from their play. In many cases, on turning for one last look as they crossed the ridge, they saw their homes in flames, fired by the lawless rabble that followed on the heels of the soldiers to loot and pillage. So keen were these outlaws on the scent that in some instances they were driving off the cattle and other stock of the Indians almost before the soldiers had fairly started their owners in the other direction. Systematic hunts were made by the same men for Indian graves, to rob them of the silver pendants and other valuables deposited with the dead. A Georgia volunteer, afterward a colonel in the Confederate service, said: "I fought through the civil war and have seen men shot to pieces and slaughtered by thousands, but the Cherokee removal was the cruelest work I ever knew." (Mooney [1900], 124)

John G. Burnett, a soldier who participated in the removal, describes other events.

Men working in the fields were arrested and driven to the stockades. Women were dragged from their homes by soldiers whose language they could not understand. Children were often separated from their parents and driven into the stockades with the sky for a blanket and the earth for a pillow. And often the old and infirm were prodded with bayonets to hasten them to the stockades. In one home death had come during the night, a little sad faced child had died and was lying on a bear skin couch and some women were preparing the little body for burial. All were arrested and driven out leaving the child in the cabin. I don't know who buried the body. In another home was a frail Mother, apparently a widow and three small children, one just a baby. When told that she must go the Mother gathered the children at her feet, prayed an humble prayer in her native tongue, patted the old family dog on the head, told the faithful creature good-by, with a baby strapped on her back and leading a child with each hand started on her exile. But the task was too great for that frail Mother. A stroke of heart failure relieved her sufferings. She sunk and died with her baby on her back, and her other two children clinging to her hands. (Burnett 1978, 183)

Almost 17,000 Cherokees were rounded up and put in stockades constructed on their lands for the purpose of holding them. (About 4,000 had already left Cherokee Country to make new lives in Indian Territory; around 1,000 "escaped" into the hills and mountains; some received land allotments in the Southeast.) The small groups were then gathered at three points for removal westward: at Old Agency on the Hiwassee River (near Calhoun, Tennessee); at Ross's Landing (Chattanooga, Tennessee); and at Gunter's Landing (Guntersville, Alabama).

The plan was to load the Cherokees on steamboats and move them down the Tennessee and Ohio rivers to the Mississippi, and then send them overland to Indian Territory. A few thousand Cherokees were so removed; but "this removal in the hottest part of the year, was attended with so great sickness and mortality that, by resolution of the Cherokee national council, Ross and the other chiefs submitted to General Scott a proposition that the Cherokee be allowed to remove themselves in the fall, after the sickly season had ended" (Mooney [1900], 125–26).

The request was granted. After the summer heat, the Cherokees began to remove themselves—primarily over land—in thirteen recorded groups averaging about a thousand people each (see table 1). Most traveled north and west across Tennessee and Kentucky, across southern Illinois and Missouri, and then into northeastern Indian Territory (see map 1). Deaths occurred almost every day, from disease, cold, hardship, and accidents. Rebecca Neugin made the journey as a three-year old.

When the soldier came to our house my father wanted to fight, but my mother told him that the soldiers would kill him if he did and we surrendered without a fight. They drove us out of our house to join other prisoners in a stockade. After they took us away, my mother begged them to let her go back and get some bedding. So they let her go back and she brought what bedding and a few cooking utensils she could carry and had to leave behind all of our other household possessions.

Demography of the Trail of Tears

TABLE 1
Detachments of Cherokee During Trail of Tears Removal

Detachment	Date of Departure	Number	Date of Arrival	Number
Hair Conrad	August 23, 1838	729	January 17, 1839	654
Elijah Hicks	September 1, 1838	858	January 4, 1839	744
Jesse Bushyhead	September 3, 1838	950	February 27, 1839	898
John Benge	September 28, 1838	1,200	January 17, 1839	1,132
Situwakee	September 7, 1838	1,250	February 2, 1839	1,033
Old Field	September 24, 1838	983	February 23, 1839	921
Moses Daniel	September 20, 1838	1,035	March 2, 1839	924
Choowalooka	September 14, 1838	1,150	March ?, 1839	970
James Brown	September 10, 1838	850	March 5, 1839	717
George Hicks	September 7, 1838	1,118	March 14, 1838	1,039
Richard Taylor	September 20, 1838	1,029	March 24, 1839	942
Peter Hildebrand	October 23, 1838	1,766	March 24, 1839	1,311
John Drew	December 5, 1838	231	March 18, 1839	219

Source: Emigration Detachments (King and Evans 1978, 186–87).

My father had a wagon pulled by two spans of oxen to haul us in. Eight of my brothers and sisters and two or three widow women and children rode with us. My brother Dick, who was a good deal older than I was, walked along with a long whip which he popped over the backs of the oxen and drove them all the way. My mother and father walked all the way also.

The people got so tired of eating salt pork on the journey that my father would walk through the woods as we traveled, hunting for turkeys and deer which he brought into camp to feed us. Camp was usually made at some place where water was to be had and when we stopped and prepared to cook our food, other emigrants who had been driven from their homes without opportunity to secure cooking utensils came to our camp to use our pots and kettles. There was much sickness among the emigrants and a great many little children died of whooping cough. (Neugin 1978)

Suffering and turmoil did not end on arrival in Indian Territory. Many Cherokees survived the hardships of imprisonment and travel only to face disease or starvation in the new homelands (Doran 1975–76, 499). Prob-

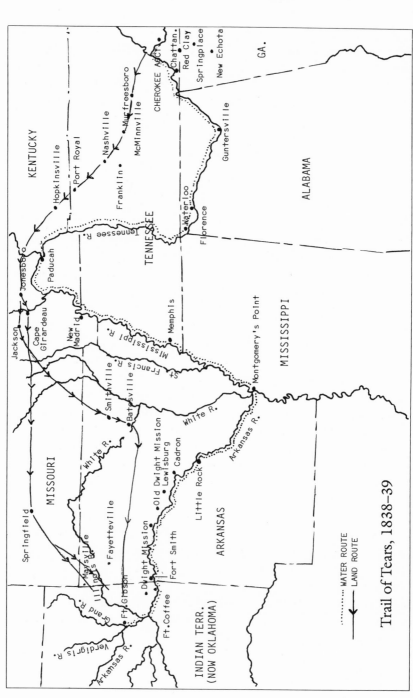

Trail of Tears, 1838–39

.... WATER ROUTE
⟵ LAND ROUTE

Map 1.

ably in part because of the severity of the relocation, three of the Cherokee men who had signed the Treaty of New Echota—Major Ridge, his son John Ridge, and Elias Boudinot—were executed. "The men were killed in accordance with the law of the Nation—three times formulated, and still in existence—which made it treason, punishable with death, to cede away lands except by act of the general council of the Nation" (Mooney [1900], 128).

CURRENT VIEW OF POPULATION LOSSES

Thousands of Cherokees are said to have died during the entire Trail of Tears ordeal; that is, during the roundup and the months spent in stockades awaiting removal, during the journeys themselves, and during the first year in Indian Territory. Sicknesses and diseases they suffered included colds, influenza, sore throat, pleurisy, measles, diarrhea, fevers, toothache, and, among the young men, gonorrhea (Knight 1954–55, 424), as well as dysentery (Howard and Allen 1975–76, 352–54), whooping cough, and cholera (Foreman 1932, 238–312). Others died as a result of accidents, cold of winter, hardships of the journey, and shots from soldiers' rifles; still others from inadequate food and starvation (Foreman 1932, 238–312; Mooney [1900], 124–30).

As mentioned, many deaths occurred neither prior to nor during the removal, but soon after arrival in Indian Territory. According to information derived from sources on the Five Civilized Tribes soon after their arrival, "it would seem that the great majority managed to reach their homelands. However, soon afterward they were swept by a series of epidemic disease, and it was then that a tremendous number died" (Doran 1975–76, 497). Although there are no estimates available for the Cherokee death rate, "they began dying in great numbers soon after arrival, for they had no doctors or medicine to combat disease . . . many died of simple starvation . . . , because of blatant corruption among the agents at the supply depots" (Doran 1975–76, 498).

No detailed information is available as to exactly how many Cherokee died during the ordeal; only speculations exist. However, there is high consensus on a figure. In writing on Cherokee relocation, Mooney commented:

It is difficult to arrive at any accurate statement of the number of Cherokee who died as the result of the Removal. According to the official
figures those who removed under the direction of Ross lost over 1,600
on the journey. The proportionate mortality among those previously
removed under military supervision was probably greater, as it was their
suffering that led to the proposition of the Cherokee national officers to
take charge of the emigration. Hundreds died in the stockades and the
waiting camps, chiefly by reason of the rations furnished, which were
of flour and other provisions to which they were unaccustomed and
which they did not know how to prepare properly. Hundreds of others
died soon after their arrival in Indian Territory, from sickness and expo-
sure on the journey. Altogether it is asserted, probably with reason, that
over 4,000 Cherokee died as the direct result of the removal. (Mooney
[1900], 127)

The figure of 4,000 deaths has generally been accepted by more recent
scholars. Foreman (1932, 312) asserts that "all told, 4,000 died during the
course of capture and detention in temporary stockades and the removal
itself"; Howard and Allen (1975–76, 354) state that "more than 4,000 eastern Cherokee died during the removal or within a year of their arrival in
the west"; and Knight (1954–55, 425) indicates that "by the time the trans-
plantation was completed in 1830, approximately four thousand Cherokees
had died."

A similar figure is given when scholars place mortality in the context of
Cherokee population estimates, either the approximately 16,000 removed
or the total tribal number of more than 20,000, which includes early emigrants west as well as those who escaped removal. Thus, Blue (1974, v)
writes, "It is commonly noted that 16,000 Cherokees were removed, 4,000
of whom died on what is called the 'Trail of Tears.'" And Swanton (1946,
113) asserts that Cherokee removal caused "intense suffering on the part of
the Indians and the loss of nearly one-fourth of their numbers." The number lost in this case would be either 4,000 or 5,000, depending on whether
Swanton was referring to the 16,000 removed or the total of 20,000.

The source of Mooney's figure of 4,000 is not known. I have located
two mentions of the figure prior to Mooney's report of it in 1900. One is
in a letter written in 1890 by a soldier who, as a young man, participated in

the removal. He writes of the "four-thousand silent graves reaching from the foothills of the Smoky Mountains to what is known as Indian Territory in the West" (Burnett 1978, 182). An earlier mention, and perhaps the original, dates from 1839, as cited in Wilkins (1970, 315). "No one knew exactly how many Cherokees had perished in the ordeal. The trail was especially hard on babies, children, and the aged. Four thousand, nearly one fifth of the entire Cherokee population, is the estimate usually cited, one made by Dr. Butler the Missionary."

Such estimates would place Cherokee mortality about midway in the mortality losses of the other four major southeastern tribes, as well as can now be ascertained. The Choctaws are said to have lost 15 percent of their population, 6,000 out of 40,000 (Allen 1970, 62), and the Chickasaws' removal is said to have been "a comparatively tranquil affair" (Foreman 1932, 226), though they surely suffered severe losses as well. By contrast, the Creeks and Seminoles are said to have suffered about 50 percent mortality (Doran 1975–76, 499–500). For the Creeks, this came primarily in the period immediately after removal. For example, "of the 10,000 or more who were resettled in 1836–37 . . . an incredible 3,500 . . . died of 'bilious fevers'" (Doran 1975–76, 497). The high Seminole mortality seems to have resulted primarily not from postremoval disease but from "the terrible war of attrition that had been required to force them to move" (Doran 1975–76, 498).

Nonetheless, the figure of 4,000 deaths during the Cherokee Trail of Tears seems highly speculative. It appears to be only a suggested estimate, one without a hard factual basis, but one that subsequent scholars have cited and recited. The exact number of Cherokee lives the removal cost was surely never known and perhaps will never be known. That information was never ascertained, never recorded, and is perhaps lost forever. It is possible, however, to derive empirically an estimate of Cherokee population losses, one based on demographic analysis using factual data.

CHEROKEE POPULATION LOSSES

It is fundamental in demography that a constantly defined population's size increases or decreases because of change in only three variables: its births, deaths, and migrations. If more individuals are born in or migrate into the defined population than die in or migrate out of it, that population increases. And if fewer individuals are born in or migrate into the population than die in or migrate out of it, that population decreases. This may be expressed in simple equation

$$P_{T2} = P_{T1} = (B - D) + (I - E)$$

where P_{T2} is population size at time two, P_{T1} is population size at time one, B is births, D is deaths, I is immigrants (those migrating into a population), and E is emigrants (those migrating out of a population).

Often, change in population size is a result only of changes in rates of births and deaths within it—migrations are not a factor, or only a very small one. Changes in population size resulting from changing birth and death rates alone are called natural increases and natural decreases. Similarly, natural increases or decreases of a defined population occur either because of change in rates of births or deaths or change in rates of both births and deaths. Population decline by natural decrease may, therefore, be a result of either higher death rates, lower birth rates, or some combination of change in both.

A New Perspective

In an important sense, the often-cited 4,000 mortality figure encompasses only one perspective of Cherokee population loss due to removal. From another perspective one may speak of *total* Cherokee population losses. In this sense, population loss is the difference between actual population size (after removal) and what population size would have been had removal not occurred. This calculation is based not only on increased death rates during the removal, but also on changes in the frequency both of birth and of migration, the two other components of numerical population change. Removal surely affected fertility and migration as well as mortality; effects on both should be included, therefore, along with effects on mortality in estimating a total population cost for the Trail of Tears. It is this perspective that guides the following estimate of Cherokee population losses during their removal.

Demography of the Trail of Tears

Available Population Data

Reasonable and direct data do not exist for ascertaining a total Cherokee population loss during the entire Trail of Tears period. Cherokee population size at time of removal may be fairly accurately stated from the 1835 Cherokee census, along with estimates of earlier western emigration. Also needed, however, are mortality, fertility, and migration rates for the removal period, in order to project the 1835 population to a date subsequent to the time of removal, *and* a population enumeration for the same date with which to compare this population projection. None of these are available, it seems. Nevertheless, it is possible to approximate the two figures utilizing existing data, thus establishing a reasonable estimate of total Cherokee population loss during the period of the Trail of Tears.

Various records and estimates of Cherokee population size are available for points throughout the nineteenth century. These range from the Meigs census of 1809, which reported 12,395 eastern Cherokees (McLoughlin and Conser 1977), to the 1890 United States census enumeration of 22,015 Western Cherokees (U.S. Bureau of the Census 1894).

As mentioned above, a Cherokee census was undertaken in 1835, shortly before the United States government started to remove the Cherokees in 1837. It enumerated 16,542 Eastern Cherokees; there were already an estimated 5,000 Cherokees west of the Mississippi, most of whom had emigrated during the preceding two decades (McLoughlin and Conser 1977, 702). Prior to this, there was the Meigs census in 1809, a census reported by Boudinot in 1826, and the *Cherokee Phoenix* census of 1828.

The next dates for which reasonably good population data exist do not occur until after 1850. The 1840 census by William Holland Thomas and the 1848 Mullay roll of North Carolina Cherokees do not appear to be complete enough to use. However, the Drennen roll, taken in 1852, is usable (Doran 1975–76, 500) and seems a fairly complete count of the Western Cherokees. To it may be added an adjusted 1851 figure for Eastern Cherokees from the Siler census (see table 2). In 1867,[1] there was another census of Western Cherokees, reported by Royce (1975, 229), which is also reliable. After this point, United States census enumerations are available for dates throughout the remainder of the nineteenth century; these include both enumerations of Western Cherokees and estimates of the numbers of Eastern Cherokees.

TABLE 2
Cherokee Population Size, 1808–9 to 1880

Date	Eastern	Western	Total
1808–9	12,395 [a]	1,000 [b]	13,395
1826	13,963 [c]	3,500–4,000 [c]	17,713
1828	14,972 [d]	3,500–4,000 [c](?)	18,722
1835	16,542 [f]	5,000 [g](?)	21,542
1851–52	1,981 [h](?)	13,821 [i]	15,802
1867	2,000 [i](?)	13,566 [k]	15,566
1875	2,500 [l]	17,217 [l]	19,717
1880	2,200 [l]	19,720 [l]	21,920

[a] Meigs Census (cited in McLoughlin and Conser 1977, 681).
[b] Baker (1977).
[c] Boudinot figure (cited in McLoughlin and Conser 1977, 681).
[d] *Cherokee Phoenix* figure (cited in McLoughlin and Conser 1977, 681).
[e] This is for the year 1826.
[f] Cherokee Census of 1835 (Tyner 1974).
[g] McLoughlin and Conser (1977, 702).
[h] Eastern Cherokee Census of 1851 (Siler 1972). The total number of names is 2,343; however, 363 of these were whites and other disallowed individuals, and one individual was skipped in the numbering (see Royce [(1887), 192] for additional information).
[i] Drennen Roll (cited in Doran 1975–76).
[j] Estimated.
[k] Royce ([1887], 229).
[l] U.S. Bureau of the Census (1915, 83).

Given the availability of these various population data, it is possible to obtain the desired two estimates of Cherokee population size for a common date of interest. This may be accomplished by projecting *forward* the population trend culminating with the 1835 census and projecting *backward* the trend beginning with the 1852 roll. The projections will provide an estimate of the actual Cherokee population size immediately after removal and an estimate of the hypothetical Cherokee population size had removal not occurred. By comparing the two estimates, Cherokee population loss due to removal can be estimated.

The only detail remaining is the selection of a postremoval date for the population estimates. The most appropriate date seems to be 1840. Actual removal ended in 1839, but apparently its immediate effects continued for at least a year afterward. It will be recalled that the 4,000 deaths attributed to removal are said by some to cover the span of capture, detention, and relocation of the Cherokees and the year thereafter (Foreman 1932, 312; Howard and Allen 1975–76, 354),[2] although the estimate seems to have first been made in 1839 and would not have included postremoval losses. Thus, the date 1840 will be used to mark the end of the removal period.

To obtain the two estimates, Cherokee population sizes for three nineteenth-century points prior to the 1835 Census and three following the 1852 roll were established from the censuses and rolls named above. Included in all instances were population sizes for both Eastern and Western Cherokees, since the tribal population had been divided as of the late eighteenth century. This enables a total size of the Cherokee population to be established for all dates (see table 2).

After establishing these data points, the two sets of figures were examined to ascertain how closely each follows a mathematical curve. (The main discrepancy is for 1867, immediately after the Civil War. The Cherokees suffered severe population losses from the war; hence, the small population decline from 1851–52 to 1867 [Mooney (1900), 149].[3] Because the

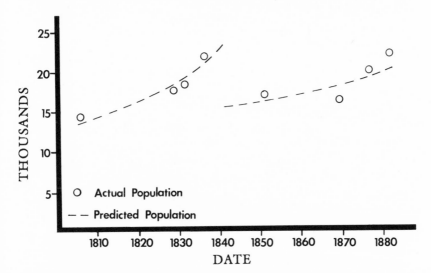

Actual Cherokee population sizes and predicted population curves, 1808–9 to 1840, 1880 to 1840.

TABLE 3
*Actual and Predicted Cherokee
Population Size, 1808–9 to 1840,
1880 to 1840*

Date	Actual	Predicted[a]
1808–9	13,395	13,292
1826	17,713	18,100
1828	18,722	18,750
1835	21,542	21,214
1840	—	23,170
1840	—	13,080
1851–52	15,802	14,906
1867	15,566	17,777
1875	19,717	19,469
1880	21,920	20,607

[a] From the formula $\log y = a + bx$, where y is population, a is y-intercept, b is slope, and x is date.

data points do closely follow curves, population projections may be made from them.

Population Loss from Projections

It is now a straightforward task to obtain the desired estimates by extending the earlier logarithmic curve forward to 1840 and the later one backward to 1840. This may be done using the standard formula

$$\log y = a + bx$$

where y is population size, a is y-intercept, b is slope, and x is date.

Solving the equation for the year 1840 using the 1808–9 to 1835 population trend yields a population estimate of 23,170. Solving the equation for the same year using the 1851–52 to 1880 population trend yields a population estimate of 13,080 (see table 3). In other words, if the 1808–9 to 1835 Cherokee population trend had continued until 1840, there would have been 23,170 Cherokees in 1840; conversely, if the Cherokee population trend from 1840 to 1851–52 had been the same as from 1851–52 to 1880, there would have been only 13,080 Cherokees in 1840.

Subtracting the smaller (13,080) from the higher (23,170) estimate yields a difference of 10,090. This may be considered total Cherokee population "loss" over the five years from 1835 to 1840, that is, the Trail of Tears period.

Implications of Vital Events Estimates

Corroboration of this difference can be derived from vital events records, as well as an indication of the relative contributions of fertility and mortality. Data are not available to establish these with certainty: to do so, rates of births and deaths both before and during the removal years would need to be known, but they are not. However, fertility and mortality rates during the period can be estimated from information in written records of the Trail of Tears.

Most Cherokees were removed in thirteen groups of approximately 1,000 each during 1838–39, under the direction of their chief, John Ross. Though there is some discrepancy between counts, around 13,000 Cherokees were relocated during this time; only a few thousand were relocated during preceding years (Foreman 1932, 300). For ten of these thirteen groups, numbers of births and deaths were recorded (King and Evans 1978, 186–87). From these data, rates can be ascertained and projected across the total year. Both crude birth and death rates can be derived from the formula

$$CR = \frac{B \text{ or } D}{P} \times K$$

where B or D is births or deaths, P is population at midpoint of journey, and K is a constant of 1,000. These rates may then be converted to yearly estimates, based on 365 days from the average relocation journey of 153 days.

Assuming rates were constant during the period of removal, it is possible to ascertain the total number of births and deaths. Of course, an argument that the rates were constant or even nearly so may be tenuous. Extensive disruption in the Cherokee Nation probably did not occur until around 1837. The birth rate was probably higher and the death rate probably lower prior to this date. Yet the mortality rate was apparently higher than this for the year after the removal because of severe epidemics and starvation in Indian Territory: as we have seen, it has been asserted that most population loss occurred then (Foreman 1932, 263; Doran 1975–76, 499). It is also likely that the birth rate was lower because of epidemics and starvation. On the whole, rates may very well have averaged out; therefore, rates during actual removal may approximate the real averages of the total five-year period.

There were 69 births among the 8,884 emigrants in the ten parties reporting. These occurred during an average journey of 153 days, from departure points in the Southeast to arrival points in Indian Territory. The above formula converts this to a yearly crude birth rate of 19 per 1,000. The number of deaths reported for these same ten groups during the same period was 424.[4] This corresponds to a yearly crude death rate of 117 per 1,000. Subtracting births per 1,000 from deaths per 1,000 indicates that Cherokee population was declining at a rate of 98 per 1,000 per year.

Extending the birth and death rates to the five-year period 1835 to 1840 on the basis of the 1835 population of 21,542, it is clear that the Cherokees would have declined to 12,862 by 1840, if these rates had been constant. This is very close to the 13,080 population estimate obtained above through projected curves. Extending the rates also indicates 1,682 births and 10,362 deaths during the five-year period.

The number of "deserters" (or "emigrants") was available from the emigration rolls along with births and deaths, but only for three groups. Because of these scanty data and because many such deserters may have eventually returned and been counted among Eastern or Western Cherokees, migration rates comparable to birth and death rates were not calculated. During this period the Cherokee lost emigrants who settled along the Trail of Tears in Illinois, Indiana, Missouri, and Arkansas. However, this loss may have been offset by immigrants gained, for example, through the adoption of 985 Delawares in 1867, some Munsees (Royce [1887], 235), and 770 Shawnees in 1860 (Royce [1887], 236).

Demography of the Trail of Tears

CONCLUSIONS

The analysis indicates that the demographic devastation of Cherokee removal was far more severe than has yet been realized. Over 10,000 additional Cherokees would have been alive sometime during the period 1835 to 1840 had Cherokee removal not occurred. Not all of this population loss represents deaths, to be sure; a number of nonbirths (those that would be expected statistically that did not occur) were involved undoubtedly, as were some number of lost migrants. One must remember, too, that many Cherokees, perhaps a few thousand, would have died anyway during the time period had removal not occurred. Nevertheless, the five-year mortality estimate of 10,362 suggests that Cherokee deaths directly due to removal far exceeded the number of 4,000 generally accepted by contemporary scholars. A total mortality figure of 8,000 for the Trail of Tears period, twice the supposed 4,000, may not be at all unreasonable.

NOTES

Portions of this paper have appeared previously in Thornton (1984).

1. The census was authorized in 1866, but taken in 1867 (Royce [1887], 229).

2. Of course, subsequent effects on population could be carried forward beyond this time, even to today and into the future. Since so many other events have affected Cherokee population, projecting the population very far forward becomes meaningless.

3. Cherokees in Indian Territory formally sided with the Confederacy in the Civil War. However, the Cherokees were factionalized, and individual Cherokee fought on both sides in the war. The result was disastrous for them. Charles C. Royce describes the effects of the Civil War on the Cherokees: "Raided and sacked alternately, not only by the Confederate and Union forces, but by the vindictive ferocity and hate of their own factional divisions, their country became a blackened and desolate waste. Driven from comfortable homes, exposed to want, misery, and the elements, they perished like sheep in a snow storm. Their houses, fences, and other improvements were burned, their orchards destroyed, their flocks and herds slaughtered or driven off, their schools broken up, and their schoolhouses given to the flames, and their churches and public buildings subjected to a similar fate, and that entire portion of their country which had been occupied by their settlements was distinguishable from the virgin prairie only by the scorched and blackened chimneys and the plowed but now neglected fields" (Royce [1887], 254). James

Mooney asserted that the Cherokee population in Indian Territory declined by 7,000 as a result of the five-year Civil War—from 21,000 to 14,000—and that the war left "their whole country in ashes" (Mooney [1900], 149; see also U.S. Bureau of the Census 1894, 276, 281–82). Smallpox also continued to infect the Cherokees, particularly in 1865–66, immediately after the Civil War, and in 1899–1900 (Stearn and Stearn 1945, 101, 113–14).

4. This figure of 424 deaths departs markedly from the assertion by James Mooney ([1900], 127) that 1,600 were "lost" during the actual journey. Mooney's figure is based on records of Cherokees departing and Cherokees arriving, not on deaths during the journey (see King and Evans 1978, 186–87).

REFERENCES

ALLEN, VIRGINIA R. 1970. "Medical Practices and Health in the Choctaw Nation, 1831–1885." *Chronicles of Oklahoma* 48:124–43.

BAKER, JACK D., trans. 1977. *Cherokee Emigration Rolls, 1817–1835.* Oklahoma City: Baker Publishing.

BLUE, BRANTLEY. 1974. Foreword. In *The Indian Removals,* vol. 1, iii–v. New York: AMS Press.

BURNETT, JOHN G. 1978. "The Cherokee Removal Through the Eyes of a Private Soldier." *Journal of Cherokee Studies* 3:180–85 (special issue).

DORAN, MICHAEL F. 1975–76. "Population Statistics of Nineteenth Century Indian Territory." *Chronicles of Oklahoma* 53:492–515.

DUFFY, JOHN. 1951. "Smallpox and the Indians in the American Colonies." *Bulletin of the History of Medicine* 25:324–41.

FOREMAN, GRANT. 1932. *Indian Removal.* Norman: Oklahoma University Press.

HOWARD, R. PALMER, AND VIRGINIA R. ALLEN. 1975–76. "Stress and Death in the Settlement of Indian Territory." *Chronicles of Oklahoma* 53:352–59.

KING, DUANE H., AND E. RAYMOND EVANS, eds. 1978. "The Trail of Tears: Primary Documents of the Cherokee Removal." *Journal of Cherokee Studies* 3:129–90 (special issue).

KNIGHT, OLIVER. 1954–55. "Cherokee Society Under the Stress of Removal." *Chronicles of Oklahoma* 32:414–28.

MCLOUGHLIN, WILLIAM G., AND WALTER H. CONSER, JR. 1977. "The Cherokee in Transition: A Statistical Analysis of the Federal Cherokee Census of 1835." *Journal of American History* 54:678–703.

MOONEY, JAMES. 1928. "The Aboriginal Population of America North of Mexico." In *Smithsonian Miscellaneous Collections,* vol. 80, edited by John R. Swanton, 1–40. Washington, D.C.

Demography of the Trail of Tears

————. [1900] 1975. *Historical Sketch of the Cherokee*. Reprint. Chicago: Aldine Publishing.

NAM, CHARLES B., AND SUSAN GUSTAVUS PHILLIBER. 1984. *Population*. 2d ed. Englewood Cliffs, N.J.: Prentice-Hall.

NEUGIN, REBECCA. 1978. "Memories of the Trail." *Journal of Cherokee Studies* 3:176 (special issue).

O'DONNELL, JAMES M., III. 1973. *Southern Indians in the American Revolution*. Knoxville: University of Tennessee Press.

PRUCHA, FRANCIS PAUL. 1975. *Documents of United States Indian Policy*. Lincoln: University of Nebraska Press.

ROYCE, CHARLES C. [1887] 1975. *The Cherokee Nation of Indians*. Reprint. Chicago: Aldine Publishing.

SILER, DAVID W., comp. 1972. *The Eastern Cherokees: A Census of the Cherokee Nation in North Carolina, Tennessee, Alabama, and Georgia in 1851*. Cottonport, La.: Polyanthos.

STEARN, E. WAGNER, AND ALLEN E. STEARN. 1945. *The Effect of Smallpox on the Destiny of the Amerindian*. Boston: Bruce Humphries.

SWANTON, JOHN R. 1946. *The Indians of the Southeastern United States*. Washington, D.C.: Government Printing Office.

THORNTON, RUSSELL. 1984. "Cherokee Population Losses During the Trail of Tears: A New Perspective and a New Estimate." *Ethnohistory* 31:289–300.

————. *The Cherokees: A Population History of a People*. Lincoln: University of Nebraska Press (in press).

TYNER, JAMES W., ed. 1974. *Those Who Cried: The 16,000: A Record of the Individual Cherokees Listed in the United States Official Census of the Cherokee Nation Conducted in 1835*. Chi-ga-u.

U.S. BUREAU OF THE CENSUS. 1894. *Extra Census Bulletin. The Five Civilized Tribes in Indian Territory: The Cherokee, Chickasaw, Choctaw, Creek, and Seminole Nations*. Washington, D.C.: U.S. Census Printing Office.

————. 1915. *Indian Population in the United States and Alaska, 1910*. Washington, D.C.: Government Printing Office.

WILKINS, THURMAN. 1970. *Cherokee Tragedy*. New York: Macmillan.

The Impact of Removal on the North Carolina Cherokees

JOHN R. FINGER

Cherokee removal is one of the most infamous events in the history of Indian-white relations. The spectacle of a people being evicted from their homeland is even more poignant because the Cherokees were widely perceived as being more progressive than other Indian tribes, as having made great strides toward the white man's "civilization." Most of the literature on the Cherokees naturally focuses on this dramatic dichotomy: a people who made every effort to reshape their culture into an image that would appear pleasing to whites and who were nonetheless deported westward over the Trail of Tears. That simply makes their dispossession even more tragic, and who can resist such a scenario?

But perhaps it is time to look at removal more closely and to avoid such appealing oversimplifications. One way of doing this is to avoid perceiving the Cherokees as a unified, almost monolithic entity and to emphasize local and regional differences that helped determine how removal affected them. This paper deals with the immediate and long-term impact of the removal crisis on the North Carolina Cherokees. The crisis began, of course, with the fraudulent Treaty of New Echota, signed by a tiny minority of Cherokees in December 1835 and ratified in May 1836. It provided that within two years of its ratification the Cherokee Nation would give up its homelands in North Carolina, Georgia, Alabama, and Tennessee and emigrate to present-day Oklahoma.

A tribal census of 1835 showed 3,644 Cherokees in North Carolina out of a total of 16,542 residing east of the Mississippi. The majority of the North Carolina Indians lived within the bounds of the Cherokee Nation along the Hiwassee, Valley, and Cheoah rivers in the extreme western part of the state, with perhaps a few hundred more residing just outside the nation.[1] Fifty-one of the latter had taken advantage of clauses in the treaties of 1817 and 1819 allowing certain individuals and their families to separate from the nation and occupy private reservations on lands ceded to the United States. They claimed to be citizens of North Carolina, but their precise status was in fact uncertain. Unfortunately, whites had already intruded on many of these private reservations, and during the 1820s North Carolina negotiated cash settlements with most of the Indian reservees. Some moved back to the Cherokee Nation while others clustered around a site known as Quallatown, near where Soco Creek joins the Oconaluftee River. Their chief was an imposing individual named Yonaguska (Drowning Bear), who in turn often relied on a local white merchant, William Holland Thomas. Thomas had been adopted into the tribe while a boy and by the early 1830s had become their trusted adviser.[2]

Both groups of North Carolina Cherokees—the tribal majority and those claiming state citizenship—were more traditionalist and had fewer material possessions and white skills than most other tribal members. Practically every white visitor commented on this, including Gen. John Wool, who commanded American forces during the preparatory stages of removal. There was also less missionary activity among these people than in other parts of the Cherokee domain, although the Reverend Evan Jones and his associates labored mightily to convert them to the Baptist faith.[3]

Those North Carolina Indians still within the Cherokee Nation were staunch supporters of Principal Chief John Ross in his efforts to prevent ratification of the Treaty of New Echota and, afterwards, to resist actual removal. They were supported by the Reverend Mr. Jones, the most active of all missionaries in steadfastly opposing enforced removal. Most of these Indians refused to abide by the treaty right up to the day they were actually forced to leave at bayonet point.[4]

The other North Carolina Cherokees, those under Yonaguska and Thomas near Quallatown, were less indignant about the treaty but feared the federal government might try to apply it to them as well as the Cherokee Nation. Following the advice of Yonaguska, who told them that it would not be long before the government would demand the lands in Oklahoma, too, they intended to remain. They had a twofold argument against their possible removal: first, that their supposed citizenship exempted them from deportation; and second, that regardless of whether they were citizens, article twelve of the treaty allowed certain Cherokees to remain in their homeland. According to the article as originally agreed upon in December 1835:

> Those individuals and families of the Cherokee nation that are averse to a removal to the Cherokee country west of the Mississippi and are desirous to become citizens of the States where they reside and such as are qualified to take care of themselves and their property shall be entitled to receive their due portion of all the personal benefits accruing under this treaty for their claims, improvements and percapita . . .
>
> Such heads of Cherokee families as are desirous to reside within the States of No. Carolina, Tennessee and Alabama subject to the laws of the same; and who are qualified or calculated to become useful citizens shall be entitled . . . to one hundred and sixty acres of land or one quarter section."[5]

What did this article mean by requiring an Indian to be "qualified" to remain? Who would decide? Later, a committee was appointed to evaluate those Indians who wished to be certified as qualified, but it was most likely very strict in assessing their applications.

Another complication was the way the ratified treaty excluded the original provision in article twelve granting qualified Cherokees their own quarter sections of land. President Andrew Jackson had insisted on such an exclusion, apparently believing its practical effect would be to force *all* Cherokees to leave the Southeast. Besides, as Jackson no doubt realized, earlier grants of private allotments had caused endless difficulties and still failed to prevent Indian dispossession by unscrupulous whites.[6] This change in article twelve gave the Cherokees an unpleasant choice: to leave or, if qualified to remain, to buy their own property. Although North Carolina did not prohibit Cherokee ownership of land (despite what some scholars have claimed), few Indians possessed the means necessary to acquire any. Not surprisingly, the vast majority of Indians there, about 2,500, eventually left.

But Jackson's alteration of article twelve did not force all Cherokees to leave, as he had hoped. Those at Quallatown who claimed state citizenship steadfastly maintained their right to stay, whether qualified or not. Yet they and other Cherokees wishing to remain faced disaster unless they had an effective spokesman who could defend their rights and also acquire a land base for them. This is why the Quallatown people, along with several small groups within the Cherokee Nation, decided to send William Thomas to Washington to participate in the negotiations preceding ratification of the removal treaty. According to a power of attorney dated January 31, 1836, Thomas was "to attend to their Business" with the United States and with the other Cherokees. Although it did not specifically instruct him to defend their right to stay, it was obvious that was his main purpose. He was also to collect all monies due his clients under the pending treaty and to use it to buy them land, with the stipulation that it should be conveyed in such a way to prevent its being sold. (This, incidentally, was a justification for Thomas's keeping land titles in his own name; that way it would presumably be harder for the Indians to lose their property. Much later this had ironic and near tragic consequences.) He was also to buy a mill, blacksmithing tools, and books for the Indians and to have printed in the Cherokee language some of the laws of North Carolina. The latter reveals an obvious desire among the Indians to be familiar with their legal situation. Finally, he was to buy two hundred bushels of corn for the Indians' use the following summer. Any money left over was to go to Thomas for his expenses and services.[7]

In carrying out his major purpose in going to Washington, Thomas argued forcefully that his clients should be allowed to remain in North Carolina—the Quallatown Indians because they were already supposed citizens and the others because they were qualified to become citizens under article twelve. He also claimed that his clients were entitled to a proportionate share of all treaty benefits for giving up their interest in the tribal domain that was being ceded. Both the officials within the Office of Indian Affairs and the members of the so-called treaty party of the Cherokees agreed to his requests.[8] After that, Thomas and his clients were no longer necessarily opposed to the treaty; in fact, one may even assume that many favored it because they expected—or hoped—to remain in their homeland and still receive a share of the proceeds from sale of the Cherokee Nation. They could have their cake and eat it, too.

Thomas, it should be emphasized, was not necessarily opposed to removal of his clients, as long as it was strictly voluntary. In the fall of 1836 he assembled the Quallatown Indians and again asked whether they wished to move westward or remain in North Carolina. Finally he posted two men a few feet apart and directed those who wanted to remain to pass between them. With no hesitation, everyone did so. They would entrust themselves to Yonaguska, Thomas, the law, and a lingering hope for justice in American society.[9]

The United States government expected that between 1836 and May 1838 the Cherokee Nation would be preparing itself for emigration to the West. Chief Ross and most other tribal leaders, however, continued to resist imminent removal, resorting to a campaign of active, yet nonviolent resistance, similar in some respects to the civil rights campaigns of Martin Luther King, Jr., in this century. Ross denounced the Treaty of New Echota as a fraud, stressed Cherokee rights under previous treaties, and as further justification for being allowed to remain in their homeland, pointed to the advances in civilization among the Cherokee Nation.[10]

The Quallatown Indians, by contrast, were quietly trying to avoid controversy. William Thomas was busy buying up thousands of acres of generally poor land in present-day Jackson, Swain, Cherokee, and Macon counties for their use and for any other Cherokees qualified under article twelve to remain. At the request of the Reverend John Schermerhorn, the man who had engineered the notorious Treaty of New Echota, Thomas also spent several thousand dollars procuring corn and other necessities for Indians in western North Carolina.[11] Amid the chaos of the removal crisis many Cherokees had not devoted enough attention to the immediate problem of raising sufficient crops to survive.

Despite his clients' legal rights, Thomas left nothing to chance. In fact, his efforts on behalf of his Indian friends resembled those of John Ross in support of the Cherokee Nation. Like Ross, Thomas organized a carefully calculated campaign to convince federal and state officials that the Quallatown Indians were good, progressive people—citizens, in fact—who had both a moral and a legal right to remain. He persuaded local groups of whites to sign memorials and petitions attesting to the pacific nature of the Indians and to their recent advances in civilization under Thomas's tutelage. The Indians themselves asked North Carolina to extend its jurisdiction over them, noting that the state had always been just in its treatment of them.[12] In January 1837 the North Carolina General Assembly tacitly acknowledged the right of these Indians to stay, but carefully refrained from acknowledging them as citizens. Meanwhile some sixty Quallatown heads of families, no doubt at the prodding of Thomas, claimed they were citizens and asked the federal government to allow them to remain. Federal commissioners gave preliminary approval in September 1837 but deferred final endorsement.[13]

Some whites viewed Thomas with considerable suspicion, including at least one staunch defender of the Indians. The Reverend Mr. Jones wrote to Chief Ross about Thomas's activities, voicing the opinion that the merchant was possibly defrauding his clients.[14] Clearly, the Quallatown Indians were now distancing themselves from Ross's authority and relying upon Thomas, who had pointed out to them that their status was different from that of the Cherokee Nation. Within a few years Thomas was even attacking the Ross family in letters to the Office of Indian Affairs, and Ross's supporters were responding in kind.[15]

By the spring of 1838 it was clear to everyone that the Cherokee Nation had no intention of leaving the Southeast unless by force. Federal and state military units under the leadership of Gen. Winfield Scott prepared to enforce the provisions of the Treaty of New Echota. Some whites in western North Carolina expressed outrage that Thomas's Indian clients claimed to be exempt from removal and charged that they were providing refuge in their mountain valley for members of the Cherokee Nation who were trying to elude the army. Letters to Gov. Edward Dudley accused Thomas of various nefarious activities and characterized his Cherokee clients as debauched, backward people who eked out a meager existence. These half-savage people, some complained, might form an alliance with disaffected members of the Cherokee Nation and pose a threat to the whites of western North Carolina. One even dramatically warned of "those merciless savages bursting forth in fury . . . like a mighty torrent . . . and overspreading that entire frontier in ruin and devastation."[16] It was apparent that many Carolinians were aware of the savage Seminole war then raging in Florida and were afraid of similar Cherokee resistance, despite John Ross's disavowal of violence.[17]

At the request of Governor Dudley, Thomas and other whites offered reassurance that there was no danger. The local Indians, according to Reuben Deacon, were as passive as they had always been (at least in recent memory). As far as he was concerned, it was much ado about nothing.[18] Thomas, however, had to be extremely circumspect in his responses to critics, for he well realized that the security of the Quallatown Cherokees ultimately depended upon the goodwill of resident whites. Much of that goodwill, unfortunately, derived not from any moral outrage over what was happening to the Cherokees but from the realization that the Indians provided a convenient, cheap source of occasional labor that Thomas could supply on demand.[19]

Despite Thomas's efforts to ensure his clients' continued residency, the question of what to do with the Quallatown Cherokees naturally arose during the army's roundup. General Scott was willing to recognize that those Indians had a peculiar legal status and were probably exempt from removal, but he tried unsuccessfully to persuade them that removal was in their best interests. Thomas mollified army officers somewhat by assuring them that the Quallatown people would not provide a refuge for those members of the Cherokee Nation who were attempting to elude the army's dragnet.[20] The Quallatown Cherokees would not be able to provide the sanctuary that was a traditional feature of tribal society. They would be in the uncomfortable position of watching their brothers being tracked down while at the same time wondering whether they themselves would remain immune from the pressures of removal.

Scott's removal of the Cherokee Nation is one of the most familiar and distressing stories in the annals of Indian-white relations. Military units rounded up thousands of Indians and temporarily incarcerated them in makeshift stockades before dispatching them westward to present-day Oklahoma. Many are the tales of Indian families being accosted in their cabins and having just a moment or two to gather a few possessions before leaving forever. In North Carolina Indians endured stifling, filthy conditions in Forts Hembrie, Delaney, Lindsay, and Butler. Many died even before embarking on the Trail of Tears. The scope of this tragedy is well known, and most North Carolina Cherokees were forced to take that long, sorrowful trail to Oklahoma. But some in the nation had secured certificates allowing them to remain, while others slipped away to the mountains and hid from the soldiers.[21]

A few Cherokees did not bother to flee but openly defied the government. Hog Bite, a hermit in Macon County who was supposedly ninety-seven years old, threatened removal agents with a gun almost as ancient as himself. They wisely decided not to test his resolve, thinking he was too old to make the trip west and would soon die anyhow. (Hog Bit fooled them. More than a decade later he was still alive and vigorous.)[22] Federal officials decided that a few other elderly Indians could also live out their final years undisturbed, but the rest of the Cherokees, except those at Quallatown and those possessing the necessary certificates, were expected to leave.

It was in this context that an improbable hero emerged in the person of a sixty-year-old member of the Cherokee Nation who was attempting to avoid deportation. His name was Tsali, but he was known to whites as Charley. Up to a point, all accounts agree on what happened. Tsali and his family were fugitives who were trying to elude the soldiers. That had been their only crime. Eventually apprehended, they were being escorted to a stockade by a detachment of several soldiers. At this point, the stories begin to differ. According to the most prevalent, the soldiers abused Tsali's ailing wife, and he suddenly produced a weapon (whether it was concealed or snatched from his startled captors is unclear), killed two of the soldiers, and escaped with his family into the mountain forests.[23] Regardless of the details, news of the incident spread like wildfire, and John Ross, then preparing to lead a detachment westward, expressed his sympathy to General Scott. He emphasized, however, that it was not something for which the entire Cherokee Nation could be held accountable. He hoped the guilty Indians would be captured and punished.[24]

Scott could not let the killings go unavenged and began a massive manhunt for the culprits. According to the most popular account, he realized it would be difficult to locate them in the mountain wilderness and thus decided to strike a deal: to offer amnesty to the few other remaining fugitives if they would assist the army in capturing Tsali and his family. Informed of this, Tsali said he did not want his people reduced to such humiliating circumstances. He voluntarily surrendered to the United States Army and, along with his brother and two sons, calmly faced certain death. As a final affront to the Cherokees, the officer in charge of the expeditionary force required the Indians themselves to perform the executions. Because of this heroic sacrifice, the story goes, Tsali's people were allowed to remain and became the progenitors of today's Eastern Band of Cherokees. This interpretation has become holy writ and is enacted every tourist season in the popular tribal pageant, *Unto These Hills*. Since its debut in 1950, nearly five million visitors have seen Tsali sanctified as a martyr and the father of his people.[25]

It appears, however, that the actual events were somewhat different from the romantic ones depicted in the pageant. While the soldiers may have abused Tsali's wife, there is no evidence that this happened. Quite possibly the killings occurred simply because Tsali and his family did not wish to be deported; this is certainly understandable and even lends another and perhaps more compelling kind of justice to their resistance. The testimony of whites indicates that it was not even Tsali who initiated the violence but, rather, his adult sons. On the other hand, there is much to suggest that General Scott did indeed offer a deal—but very discreetly and through intermediaries—whereby other fugitive Cherokees would be allowed to remain if they assisted in the pursuit of Tsali. In fact, Tsali was taken captive by these Indians after the army had left the mountains, and he and the others were indeed executed by them. There is still controversy over whether the army required them to do this or whether, as William Thomas claimed, the Indians wanted to perform this unpleasant duty because Tsali's group had endangered all Cherokees who hoped to remain. Nor is there any evidence to suggest that Tsali surrendered voluntarily, though it certainly makes a better story to say he did. Finally, most of the North Carolina Cherokees who remained, like those at Quallatown, had a legal right to do so and benefited from pursuing Tsali only in terms of showing their goodwill toward the federal government. Only those Cherokees who were fugitives from the army's dragnet profited directly from their assistance to General Scott. But perhaps one should not quibble. Regardless of the actual events, Tsali stands as an enduring and legitimate symbol of Cherokee attachment to the mountains of North Carolina and determination to remain there at all costs.[26]

In any case, by the end of 1838 the vast majority of Cherokees had been removed from the Southeast. As far as the United States government was concerned, the remaining Indians were on their own and would be subject to the sometimes not-so-tender mercies of the states in which they resided. By 1839 there were about 700 Cherokees who lived in and around Qualla-town, mostly on property that Thomas had purchased in their behalf. This number included not only the original Cherokee inhabitants of that area but also many others who legally or illegally moved there to escape removal. Among the latter was a small group of former fugitives who had served the army well in tracking down Tsali and his family.[27]

In attempting to persuade North Carolina officials to acknowledge the citizenship of the remaining Indians, William Thomas referred to various treaties and legislation, appealed for sympathy and justice, and consistently portrayed the Cherokees as progressive and well advanced in civilization. And yet, despite such claims, the Quallatown people were among the most traditionalist of all Cherokees, with an overwhelming majority classified as full bloods. English was almost unknown to them, and very few could read and write even in their own language. Predictably, they relied heavily on Thomas, and after Yonaguska died in the spring of 1839, the white man became their de facto chief, handling all official relations with their white neighbors and with state and federal officials.[28]

Another 400 or so Cherokees lived in other parts of western North Carolina, especially along the Hiwassee, Valley, and Cheoah rivers. Most of those near the Valley River were more acculturated than the others and included some mixed-bloods who had valid title to their lands. Such people were more independent in their actions than the Quallatown Cherokees and less disposed to follow the advice of Thomas. Instead, they increasingly dealt with other Cherokee agents such as Preston Starrett, Felix Axley, and Johnson K. Rogers. Those living along the Cheoah River, in contrast, were as traditionalist as the Quallatown residents and had frequent contact with them and Thomas. Their community of Buffalotown was situated near present-day Robbinsville and served as the nucleus for what became the Snowbird Community, which is still a center of traditionalism. Eventually these separate North Carolina groups coalesced into the Eastern Band.[29]

Besides the 1,100 or so Cherokees remaining in North Carolina, there were perhaps 300 in nearby parts of Georgia, Alabama, and Tennessee, making a total of about 1,400 who avoided removal. Those Indians who lived outside North Carolina were generally much more acculturated than the others, but from time to time a few moved to North Carolina or attempted to share in certain financial benefits due the North Carolina Indians.[30]

During 1841–44 the federal government attempted to persuade all remaining Cherokees in the Southeast to give up any pretense to state citizenship and consolidate with the Cherokee Nation in the West. These efforts reflected both the sincere belief of Secretary of War T. Hartley Crawford that it was in the Indians' best interest and a large measure of crass expediency. Already countless claims had been filed by both the Cherokee Nation and so-called citizen Indians for losses incurred under the Treaty of New Echota. Government officials believed it logical to settle all these claims by negotiating a new treaty, but this was impossible as long as some claimants lived apart from the Cherokee Nation as supposed citizens of the states. The obvious solution was for all Cherokees to come together in the West as members of the Cherokee Nation and then conclude a new treaty. To Crawford's chagrin, efforts to persuade more than a few North Carolina Cherokees to move proved futile.[31]

In fact, throughout the 1840s small groups of Indians wearied of life in the West and trudged back to the mountains. In January 1843 a legislative committee even expressed a fear that western North Carolina might become a haven for the "refuse" of the Cherokee Nation. In the opinion of the committee, "The mixing of these people with our white population must have a demoralizing influence which ought to be resisted by all the means within our power." It proposed a resolution asking the president to do all he could to remove the remaining Cherokees in conformity with the Treaty of New Echota. Though the North Carolina House of Commons passed the resolution, the senate tabled it. Clearly, the state of North Carolina no longer considered the Cherokee presence a momentous issue. Unlike their Georgia counterparts, whites in North Carolina were unwilling to take strong action against the relatively few, inoffensive Cherokees who lived on remote, marginal lands. In fact, the state even honored one returnee from the West, the illustrious Junaluska, who in 1814 had led Andrew Jackson's Cherokee allies against the Creeks at the battle of Horseshoe Bend. Now an old man, Junaluska was determined that when he died his bones would mingle with those of his ancestors. To its credit, the general assembly granted him citizenship and a tract of land in the mountains of Cherokee County.[32] Other Cherokees, however, would have to wait a long time for an affirmation of their citizenship.

Not until 1866, after the Cherokees had proved their loyalty to the Confederacy, did North Carolina even explicitly acknowledge the Indians' right of residency. Two years later the federal government recognized the Eastern Band as a distinct tribe under its guardianship and began helping the Indians establish a reservation from the lands purchased by Thomas, a reservation they continue to occupy. Thomas's lack of adequate records made this a time-consuming and frustrating task. In the meantime his mental and financial problems prevented him from exercising effective leadership, and rival factions of Cherokees bitterly contended with one another. Eventually the Quallatown group gained ascendancy and made the new town of Cherokee the seat of tribal government.[33]

What conclusions can we make about the impact of removal on the North Carolina Cherokees? First, it is worthwhile to stress the obvious: a minority of these Indians, through tenacity, a deep attachment to their homeland, and the considerable efforts of William Holland Thomas, were able to avoid the trauma of moving westward over the Trail of Tears. Most of those who remained had a legal right to do so, or at least argued that they did, and the United States Army never attempted to remove them. The episode involing Tsali was not a major reason the North Carolina Indians were able to remain, and yet, even today, Tsali has a profound symbolic significance for the Eastern Band.

There is another point that should be obvious. William Thomas was an essential component of the drama involving the remaining North Carolina Cherokees. It is fashionable today to attack him for various real and alleged quirks and irregularities, but it is difficult to conceive of how the Cherokees could have stayed in western North Carolina without his steadfast assistance over such a long period. It was also he who represented their interests in Washington and Raleigh and who persistently attempted to collect federal funds owed his clients under terms of various treaties. As the Indians themselves fully realized, they owed him a great deal.

A less obvious but significant feature of the removal crisis was the elimination of the provision in the original Treaty of New Echota granting quarter sections of land to those Cherokees who wished to stay. This forced the Quallatown people and some other Cherokees to rely on Thomas to purchase land for them. And since he bought land in blocks, it also forced them to cluster more closely together, to live as a tribal community at a time when the federal government was attempting to civilize Indians by getting them to give up communal landholding and live on individual tracts like whites. The United States government, paradoxically, was forcing many North Carolina Cherokees to resort to a more communal, traditional life-style.

Another important aspect of this traditionalism was the way the removal crisis heightened the North Carolina Indians' sense of being Cherokee, of being apart from other segments of society. It introduced a kind of siege mentality, an attitude of "us versus them." Both their uncertain legal status and their struggle to remain in the state (against periodic efforts to send them to Oklahoma) reinforced in the minds of many their distinctive Cherokee identity.[34] This kind of internal self-identification is as important as outward behavior and material culture in defining a tribal outlook.

In fact, one might argue that the threat of removal preserved Cherokee tribalism in North Carolina at a time when it might otherwise have faded away. This renewed sense of Cherokee identity, the necessity of acquiring a communal land base, and the tenacity in resisting complete absorption into the surrounding white society all helped preserve and even promote tribalism. And yet, paradoxically, William Thomas attempted to convince white North Carolinians that the Cherokees were worthy citizens by consistently portraying them as steadily progressing toward "civilization."[35]

Finally, it should be acknolwedged that the tenacity of the Indians and the efforts of Thomas would not have been enough to protect these people had the lands they occupied been more attractive to white settlers. Most of the remaining Cherokees lived in inaccessible and relatively unproductive areas. Looking at a map of today's Indian reservations, it is apparent that they exist only in those areas considered unattractive by whites during the nineteenth century. It is the ironic good fortune of the North Carolina Cherokees that their seemingly worthless lands now adjoin the Great Smoky Mountains National Park and yearly attract millions of tourists eager to see both mountain splendor and "real" Indians.

Impact of Removal

NOTES

1. 1835 Census (Henderson Roll), in James W. Tyner, ed., *Those Who Cried: The 16,000: A Record of the Individual Cherokees Listed in the United States Official Census of the Cherokee Nation Conducted in 1835* (Chi-ga-u, 1974). The census is also available on microfilm from the National Archives, Record Group 75, T-496, "Census Roll, 1835, of Cherokee Indians East of the Mississippi."

2. For the early history of these Indians, see John R. Finger, *The Eastern Band of Cherokees, 1819–1900* (Knoxville: University of Tennessee Press, 1984). Thomas's career is discussed in Mattie Russell, "William Holland Thomas: White Chief of the North Carolina Cherokees" (Ph.D. diss., Duke University, 1956). See also Brett H. Riggs, *An Historical and Archaeological Reconnaissance of Citizen Cherokee Reservations in Macon, Swain, and Jackson Counties, North Carolina* (Knoxville: Department of Anthropology, University of Tennessee, 1988). The North Carolina reservations consisted of forty-nine life estates and two fee simple reserves.

3. Gen. John Wool to Maj. Gen. A. Macomb, October 12, 1836, 25th Cong., 2d sess., S. Doc. 120 (Serial 315), 48. The definitive study of mission work among the Cherokees is William G. McLoughlin, *Cherokees and Missionaries, 1789–1839* (New Haven: Yale University Press, 1984).

4. Walter H. Conser, Jr., "John Ross and the Cherokee Resistance Campaigns, 1833–1838," *Journal of Southern History* 44 (May 1978): 191–212. The best biography of Ross is Gary E. Moulton, *John Ross: Cherokee Chief* (Athens: University of Georgia Press, 1978). On Evan Jones, see McLoughlin, *Cherokees and Missionaries*.

5. Charles J. Kappler, comp. and ed., *Indian Affairs: Laws and Treaties*, 5 vols. (Washington, D.C.: Government Printing Office, 1904–41), 2:444.

6. Supplementary Article I, ibid., 448. See also Mary E. Young, *Redskins, Ruffleshirts, and Rednecks: Indian Allotments in Alabama and Mississippi, 1830–1860* (Norman: University of Oklahoma Press, 1961), 191–93, and William G. McLoughlin, "Experiment in Cherokee Citizenship, 1817–1829," *American Quarterly* 33 (Spring 1981): 3–25.

7. Power of Attorney, January 31, 1836, William Holland Thomas Papers, 4 microfilm rolls, Newspapers and Microforms Department, Duke University, Durham, N.C., roll 2.

8. Commissioner of Indian Affairs C. A. Harris to William Thomas, July 19, 1836, ibid.; see also S. Doc. 120 (Serial 315), 612–17.

9. James Mooney, "Myths of the Cherokees," Bureau of American Ethnology, *Nineteenth Annual Report, 1897–98*, pt. 1 (Washington, D.C.: Government Printing Office, 1900), 163; Charles Lanman, *Letters from the Alleghany Mountains* (New York: G. P. Putnam, 1849), 109–10; Russell, "William Holland Thomas," 69.

10. Conser, "John Ross and the Cherokee Resistance Campaigns."

11. John Schermerhorn to Commissioner of Indian Affairs C. A. Harris, July 4, 1836, Thomas Papers, roll 2.

12. John R. Finger, "The North Carolina Cherokees, 1838–1866: Traditionalism, Progressivism, and the Affirmation of State Citizenship," *Journal of Cherokee Studies* 5 (Spring 1980): 17–29; Finger, *Eastern Band of Cherokees*, 18.

13. *Laws of North Carolina, 1836–37* (Raleigh, 1837), 30; *Memorial of Qualla Town Cherokees*, April 6, 1837, 29th Cong., 1st sess., S. Doc. 408 (Serial 477), 17–18.

14. Evan Jones to John Ross, November 20, 1837, in *The Papers of Chief John Ross*, ed. Gary E. Moulton, 2 vols. (Norman: University of Oklahoma Press, 1985), 1:549–51.

15. See, for example, William Thomas to Commissioner of Indian Affairs T. Hartley Crawford, October 17, 1841, Office of Indian Affairs, Letters Received, 1824–81, Record Group 75, Microcopy 234, roll 85, frames 499–501 (hereafter cited as M-234); Thomas to Acting Commissioner of Indian Affairs Daniel Kurtz, November 13, 1841, ibid., frames 509–10; Finger, *Eastern Band of Cherokees*, 31–33.

16. One of many examples in the Governors' Papers at the North Carolina Division of Archives and History (Raleigh) is M. Killian to Gov. Edward B. Dudley, March 25, 1838 (quotation), Dudley Papers.

17. Finger, *Eastern Band of Cherokees*, 20.

18. Reuben Deacon to Col. N. J. King, March 29, 1838, Dudley Papers.

19. Evidence for the Cherokees' supplying labor during this period is mostly inferential, derived from a close reading of Thomas's letters, various memorials concerning the Indians, and later known instances of Cherokee employment.

20. George E. Frizzell, "The Legal Status of the Eastern Band of Cherokee Indians" (master's thesis, Western Carolina University, 1981), 15–17.

21. Accounts of Cherokee removal are in Grant Foreman, *Indian Removal: The Emigration of the Five Civilized Tribes of Indians* (Norman: University of Oklahoma Press, 1953); Marion L. Starkey, *The Cherokee Nation* (New York: Alfred A. Knopf, 1946); and Grace Steele Woodward, *The Cherokees* (Norman: University of Oklahoma Press, 1963).

22. Lanman, *Letters from the Alleghany Mountains*, 79. Hog Bite was listed as 110 years old in 1851. David W. Siler, comp., *The Eastern Cherokees: A Census of the Cherokee Nation in North Carolina, Tennessee, Alabama, and Georgia in 1851* (Cottonport, La.: Polyanthos, 1972).

23. Extended accounts of Tsali are in Finger, *Eastern Band of Cherokees*, 21–28, and John R. Finger, "The Saga of Tsali: Legend Versus Reality," *North Carolina Historical Review* 56 (Winter 1979): 1–18.

24. John Ross to Winfield Scott, November 4, 1838, Cherokee-related materials,

National Archives, Washington, D.C. (Microfilm, Newspapers and Microforms Department, Duke University Library, Durham, N.C., roll 1).

25. Finger, *Eastern Band of Cherokees*, 21–22. Through the 1988 season paid attendance at the pageant was more than 4.6 million. *Cherokee One Feather* (Cherokee, N.C.), September 7, 1988.

26. Finger, *Eastern Band of Cherokees*, 22–28.

27. "Present state of civilization among the Cherokee Indians of Qualla Town," accompanying letter of William H. Thomas to William Wilkins, March 3, 1845, M-234, roll 89, frames 542–43.

28. Finger, *Eastern Band of Cherokees*, chaps. 3–4.

29. See the figures in William Thomas, "Census of the North Carolina Cherokees, 1840," William Holland Thomas Papers, Manuscripts Division, Duke University; compare with his "Supplementary Report of Cherokee Indians Remaining in N.C., 1835–1840" (microfilm at Museum of the Cherokee Indian, Cherokee, N.C.). For Snowbird, see Sharlotte Neely Williams, "Ethnicity in a Native American Community" (Ph.D. diss., University of North Carolina, Chapel Hill, 1976). Numerous letters in M-234 reveal the activities of Thomas and other Cherokee agents.

30. There are many letters in M-234 from Cherokees residing in Tennessee, Alabama, and Georgia.

31. Finger, *Eastern Band of Cherokees*, 31–40; for more detail, see John R. Finger, "The Abortive Second Cherokee Removal, 1841–1844," *Journal of Southern History* 47 (May 1981): 207–26.

32. Finger, *Eastern Band of Cherokees*, 37–38; James C. Mullay to Commissioner of Indian Affairs Luke Lea, January 23, 1851, M-234, roll 95, frames 624–25; act of January 2, 1847, *Laws of North Carolina, 1846–47* (Raleigh, 1847), 128.

33. Finger, *Eastern Band of Cherokees*, chaps. 6–8.

34. The frequent efforts to remove the eastern Cherokees after 1838 are discussed in Finger, *Eastern Band of Cherokees*.

35. Finger, "North Carolina Cherokees."

Beyond the Trail of Tears: One Hundred Fifty Years of Cherokee Survival

RENNARD STRICKLAND
AND WILLIAM M. STRICKLAND

At Philadelphia I was introduced to two of the Chiefs of the Cherokee Nation so sadly dealt with by the State of Georgia. . . . I never in my whole life was more affected by the consideration that they and their whole race are destined to destruction.
ASSOCIATE JUSTICE JOSEPH STORY

After casting his futile vote in their favor in *Worcester v. Georgia*, Supreme Court Justice Joseph Story publicly mourned the passing of the Cherokees.[1] Story believed, as did many Cherokees themselves, that removal would bring their tragic end. More than 150 years have passed since Story forecast the doom of this Indian nation. Today, the Cherokee Nation survives as the second largest Indian tribe in the United States, with more than 230,000 descendants by blood, 80,956 of whom are formally registered, and more than 50,000 active in some form of tribal life and lifeways. The Cherokee Nation survives, changed in many respects, but in many others as near to the Cherokees of 1838 as they were to the Cherokees of 1688. Today the tribe has no doubt that in another 150 years basic Cherokee values, deeply rooted in tribal ways, will have survived.[2]

The story of Cherokee survival is remarkable. It is the struggle of a people who, but for the extraordinary will to prevail, might have fulfilled

Story's prophesy. In the century and a half since Cherokee removal, the tribe has passed through at least six stages, each of which represented a new set of challenges.

REESTABLISHMENT OF A UNIFIED NATION, 1839–48

Removal shattered the matrix of Cherokee society. Their religion and their lifeway were intimately tied to ancestral mountains and streams. Removal ripped them from these ancient sources of strength and shook their infant institutions of government. Finally, bitter controversy divided the leadership so that two Cherokee nations came west to settle among the already established western Cherokees.

Prior to removal, the government of Chief John Ross passed a resolution carrying their government intact to the West. Their opponents, the treaty party under the leadership of Major Ridge, John Ridge, and Elias Boudinot, disputed the legitimacy of the Ross government, which had earlier suspended tribal elections. Members of the treaty party voluntarily migrated prior to the Trail of Tears migration and were settled in the new territory when Ross and his followers arrived in 1839. The internecine conflict that had smoldered in Georgia and Tennessee flared when these factions were thrown together at the trail's end. The relative prosperity of the treaty party members ignited the dormant resentments of the impoverished Cherokees who had suffered the agony of the Trail of Tears.

Cherokee civil war burst forth.[3] In June 1839, on the eve of a planned constitutional convention for reunion, the leadership of the Ridge-Boudinot group was brutally murdered. The assassins came from the rival Ross faction, but Chief John Ross himself disclaimed any involvement. For the next decade the primary tasks of the Cherokee people were to establish peace and to form a united government. The venerable Sequoyah served as president of the constitutional convention, which formally united the eastern and western Cherokee on September 6, 1839. The Act of Union had little immediate impact in restoring order.

For more than a decade the tribe fought this bloody civil war. The vaunted Cherokee respect for civil rights and government by consensus had not survived the Trail of Tears. Within the nation's borders arson and assassination were commonplace. It was almost as if a distorted version of the old clan revenge system had reemerged. The Cherokees seemed determined to destroy themselves. The court system operated amid allegations of use of the law as a political weapon against the enemies of Chief Ross. The military, particularly Commandant Matthew Arbuckle at Fort Gibson, sided with the anti-Ross Cherokees who sought to split the tribe and formally recognize two separate Cherokee nations. Division seemed inevitable. The prospect of Cherokee survival was being reduced on a daily basis. Gangs of marauders took advantage of the lawlessness; more and more Cherokees left the nation to join the Texas Cherokees or to find the California goldfields.[4]

A smoldering peace came to the Cherokee Nation after the United States government forced the tribal factions to sign a treaty of agreement in Washington in 1846. Even then, bitter partisans nursed hatreds that would erupt again when the Cherokees were drawn into the American Civil War.

CHEROKEE RENAISSANCE, 1849–60

The period between the Cherokee civil war and the American Civil War is popularly known as the "Golden Age of the Cherokee." Economic, cultural, and social institutions that had begun to flower before removal now came to fruition. The founding of educational institutions such as the Cherokee Male and Female Seminary symbolized this renaissance. Merchant families established the beginnings of briefly lived dynasties later destroyed by the Civil War. The farmer-planter life of the Deep South, supported as it was by black slavery, rested on top of a more broadly based prosperity. For many, the traditional Cherokee lifeway survived; the fire of the Keetoowah continued to perpetuate the ancient religion. Medicine doctors with special skills remained a powerful force. The Cherokee tribe became vibrant and confident again.

The nation consolidated its extraordinary advances begun in Georgia. The Cherokees revived a tribal newspaper, the *Cherokee Advocate,* and published books, pamphlets, and broadsides. Even more amazing was the progress made in education and government. The tribe established college-level education and 126 public schools, graduating men and women of talent and competency.

One often hears that the prosperity of the Cherokees in the 1850s was confined to the well-to-do mixed-bloods. The Murrell House, a stately antebellum mansion in Park Hill, reflected the elegant life-style of only a few. The double log cabin of the average Cherokee was simple by comparison. Yet traditional Indians enjoyed a standard of living as high as, if not higher than, their neighbors in Arkansas, Kansas, and Missouri. Their education was undoubtedly superior. Thus, without any aid from the United States, the Cherokees built a nation that was often described as the "Athens of the West."

Cherokee census records list land use, cattle, and other property of all tribal members. The nation's land resources were available to all its citizens, and poverty even among the most traditional was practically unknown. Economic opportunity was open to all, and the fruits thereof abounded in such measure that Cherokee wealth was not gained at the expense of other Cherokees. These were surplus-land societies where rich resources could be shared by all. The Reverend Samuel Worcester, who had migrated west with the tribe, noted: "But, it will be asked, is the improvement which has been described general among . . . the fullblooded Indians . . . or only the half-bloods? I answer that . . . I have spoken of the mass of people, without distinction. If it be asked, however, what class are most advanced—I answer, as a general thing—those of mixed blood. . . . But, though those of mixed blood are generally in the van, yet the whole mass of the people is on the march."[5]

In the midst of this renewal the Cherokees addressed old fears that continued to haunt them. If whites could drive them from Georgia, why not from this place? Again and again in this era the Cherokee and their Indian neighbors tentatively reached out to unite for their common defense. Tragically little came of these historic opportunities. In 1861, when Southerners who had turned on the Cherokees in the 1820s and 1830s found themselves squared off against their white brothers in the North, the Cherokees once again became red pawns in a white struggle.

RAVAGES OF WAR AND RECONSTRUCTION, 1861–71

Ties between the Indian administration and white Southerners had always been strong. Most federal officials among the Cherokees were citizens of southern states. At the outbreak of the Civil War, the entirety of the bureaucratic hierarchy in the Indian Territory resigned and transferred their allegiance to the Confederacy. Albert Pike, the Confederate Indian commissioner, expected the Cherokees to do likewise. Many Cherokees were slaveholders and naturally sympathetic to the Southern cause. Chief Ross and other prominent Cherokees lived lives that were, in many respects, identical to those of white Southerners. At first Ross sought to maintain neutrality, issuing a proclamation withdrawing the Cherokees from any role in the war. Geography and politics made neutrality impossible.[6]

Cherokee loyalty was divided. Soon the old treaty party was drawn to the Southern cause. Stand Watie, who had narrowly escaped assassination in 1839, became a brigadier general in the Confederate army. Chief Ross ultimately joined with the Confederate Indians, but the old chief was much relieved when he was "captured" and taken North to spend the remainder of the war living in exile in Philadelphia with the white family of his second wife. The eloquent letters between John Ross and Abraham Lincoln confirm the widely held notion that Ross always remained loyal in spirit. Tragically, neither Ross nor Lincoln survived to dictate the terms of peace.

The Cherokee Nation became a site of massive guerrilla warfare. Only occasionally did Indian troops serve in formal battles. Cherokee troops fought at the battles of Pea Ridge and Honey Springs.[7] For the Indian, starvation was a greater enemy than gunfire. Crops were burned and the large numbers of neutral Cherokees driven back and forth between Northern and Southern forces. Some fled to Texas; others to Kansas and Missouri. Three bitter winters re-created the horrors of removal itself. At the end of the war, the Cherokee Nation, like much of the South, was a burnt-over land. In July 1865 when Cherokee General Watie, the last Confederate general to surrender, returned to his family, even they had no idea where they would find food.[8]

Notwithstanding the loyalty of over 2,200 Cherokee soldiers who had served the Union, the United States adopted a hostile attitude toward the entire tribe. This posture, developed before the assassination of President Lincoln, continued through the administration of President Andrew Johnson. By punishing the whole Cherokee people, the government hoped to strip the nation of a vast portion of the fee-title property acquired at the time of removal in exchange for the Cherokee country east of the Mississippi and in Arkansas.

In September 1865, five federal commissioners convened at Fort Smith, Arkansas, to negotiate new treaties with the Five Civilized Tribes. At the next regular meeting of the commissioners, Chairman Dennis N. Cooley officially deposed Chief John Ross. The commissioners hoped to shake the confidence of the Cherokee leaders in their reliance upon former treaties by threats of forfeiture of property and accusations of treason. The adamant position of Ross, of H. D. Reese, and of other Cherokee leaders, many of whom had fought with valor in Union ranks, doomed the attempt. However, groundwork had been laid for the woes of the following year.

During the spring and summer of 1866, lengthy negotiations proceeded with two Cherokee delegations, Union and Confederate, vying for official recognition. Intrigue in Washington and at Fort Smith, where the negotiations were held, produced a document unsatisfactory to either party. The curse of tribal division had once again cost the tribe whatever slim hope rested in a united front. In the final analysis, the so-called treaty of Fort Smith, negotiated by the recognized Southern delegation, contained the seeds of the forthcoming tribal crisis.

Under the terms of the treaty, the Cherokee Nation was required to surrender land, open their territory to railroads, and begin the process that would ultimately produce statehood. The costs of this war into which the Cherokees were forced against their will were as devastating as removal itself. There would be no more negotiated treaties for the Cherokees. In 1871 Congress brought the treaty era to an end and transferred the operation of Indian affairs from the Senate, which under the Constitution approved treaties, to both House and Senate, whose joint passage was required for Indian legislation. Thus, in 1871 the fights for survival shifted from the open fields of treaty negotiation to the closed legislative halls of Congress.

The Civil War marked the end of the formative era in Cherokee history. Mature political and social institutions had emerged; public offices had established continuity; seminaries of education were reopened; the sound farming and merchant economy extended into all levels of Cherokee society; the nation became prosperous again and capable of educating its children, protecting its orphans, and punishing its criminals, at no cost whatever to the federal government. In the next decades, the last political ghosts of the removal rivalries would be put to rest as the Cherokees struggled to resist the white onslaught.

EFFORTS TO DEFEAT TRIBAL DISSOLUTION, 1872–1906

In 1872 the Missouri, Kansas, and Texas Railroad entered the Cherokee Nation.[9] With the railroad came a flood of intruders pushing for the opening of Indian lands. Thus the Cherokees once again faced a battle that echoed their earlier experience in the removal crisis of the 1830s. The Cherokees' task for the remainder of the century was to defend their domain against railroads, intruders, and territorializers. The intellectual as well as monetary resources of the Cherokee Nation were continuously strained by this fight. "Every attempt to territorialize us," the Cherokee delegation had written in 1871, "is an attempt to break down the treaty barriers which keep the speculators and railroad landgrabbers off our possessions."[10]

The cost of the campaigns to hold back the tide of the intruder drained the Cherokee treasury. The tribe was compelled to maintain a delegation in Washington at all times. The costs of this effort in 1876 exceeded $30,000. The Cherokees were bombarded by new or renewed legislation and dared not leave their interests unattended. They would defeat one bill to take their lands only to see it resurrected in the next session. The despair and disdain of the Five Tribes delegation are clear in their remonstrance of 1876. "That you may, without disgust, take to your arms the deformed babe (territorial bill) which was dropped as a bastard in your midst about eight years ago, and which since then has been shoved from one committee to another all over your Capitol, its friends now present it to you fresh from cunning fingers directed by the most fastidious taste, newly washed, powdered, perfumed and dressed. Nevertheless, its identity is easily traced. No change of dress, no new christening, can make it other than it has ever been from the day of its birth—a cheat, a fraud upon Congress, the country, and citizen population of the Indian territory."[11]

External pressures from white landgrabbers had a curative effect on the old internal Cherokee political divisions. Although not completely healed,

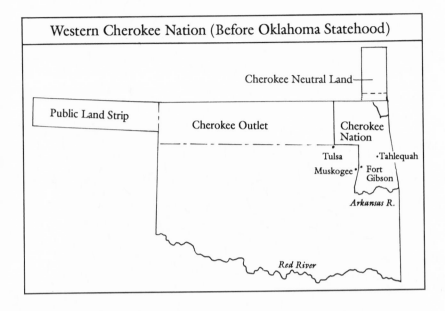

Western Cherokee Nation (Before Oklahoma Statehood)

the split became less relevant as new alliances of Civil War veterans, treaty party men, and dissatisfied Ross fullbloods realigned into the Downing Party and the National Party.[12] Increasingly, outside influences such as Evan Jones and his Baptist missionaries, who had had considerable impact on earlier tribal leadership, were relegated to secondary roles. William Potter Ross, John Ross's nephew and handpicked successor, was not strong enough to hold his uncle's empire together. The tribe broke free from the vestiges of removal politics. Ironically, the most powerful external force the railroad enlisted for the opening of Indian lands was a Cherokee, Elias Cornelius Boudinot.[13] Boudinot, working from various northern railroad centers, located the "Unassigned Lands" on former Creek and Seminole lands. This two-million-acre tract had been taken after the Civil War, ostensibly to repatriate Indians from all parts of the United States, but had never been used for that purpose. This provided the wedge used in 1889 to open the lands of Indian Territory to white settlement.

Meanwhile, in spite of these external problems, the Indian Territory and particularly the Cherokee Nation came alive with several generations of Cherokee farmers, herders, and merchants practicing their trades. The rich country to which the Cherokees had been forcibly driven in the 1820s and 1830s returned great rewards in the 1870s and 1880s. Townships and rural communities prospered. The laws of the nation reflected this new economic sophistication. Great agricultural and livestock fairs, as well as industrial and commercial meetings, were held for the entire Indian Territory. The Cherokee tribe collected payments from Texas cattle interests for the lease of their Outlet lands and thus were able to operate schools and government with no tribal taxation.[14]

All this ought to have created a lasting peace and prosperity, but the Cherokees were subject to constant harassment from intruders who sneaked onto tribal lands to steal timber and stock or to rob travelers. The roadways were not safe from marauders, bootleggers, and itinerant gamblers. Lawlessness was everywhere. The presence of white intruders placed intense pressures on the Cherokee Nation. Thousands of white squatters in their territory—eventually more than a hundred thousand—were not subject to Cherokee law enforcement. Controversies between whites and Cherokee citizens under recent United States law fell outside the jurisdiction of tribal courts. In addition, federal troops refused to remove intruders as they were required to do by law.[15]

No matter how determined their negotiators and how skilled their lobbyists, the Cherokees and the other Indians were caught on the crest of one of those great cycles that recur throughout American history. Westward expansion was an old story. The Cherokees had been caught, once before, in the earlier stages, when they had been driven by the removal forces from their ancestral southern homelands. Now they were caught in an even more destructive one. It was more determined, better organized, much faster, more efficient, and more difficult to resist. Powered not only by technological marvels, such as the railroads, the steam engine, and the mechanical harvester, the new expansion was also propelled by the go-getter spirit that infused the nation. Landless Americans from older sections and newer immigrants who had temporarily settled elsewhere demanded Indian lands. This time there was no place left to remove the Cherokee, and there was little sympathy for the preservation of a way of life that left farmlands unturned, coal unmined, and timber uncut.

Even the Cherokees who had borrowed from the Anglo-Americans were, in their way, too Indian. All their tribal lands were owned in common by the citizens of the Cherokee Nation, and much of their land lay fallow. They were especially vulnerable because they had organized as an agrarian society; land-hungry white settlers considered the Cherokee domain to be "surplus agricultural lands." Equally disturbing to the white entrepreneur was the restriction by tribal laws of the commercial exploitation of timber and mineral resources. The Cherokees' rights, both economic and political, were jealously guarded. Furthermore, portions of Cherokee agricultural lands were leased to cattlemen or used by Indian ranchers themselves, who were attacked in Congress as cattle barons who exploited fellow natives. Economic preference shown to tribal citizens was resented by whites who wanted once again to convert the riches of Cherokee lands into gold and greenbacks. The goals and the values of Cherokee civilization and those of white civilization were incompatible. And, once again, the Cherokee had foolishly taken the white at his word that what had happened in Georgia would never happen again.

The year 1889 was as devastating a year for the Cherokees in the West as the year 1829 had been for them in Georgia. In an effort to address the lawlessness and to extend law and order controls over non-Indians, Congress established a federal court for Indian Territory in 1889. That same year the dramatic Oklahoma land run opened the unassigned lands in central Oklahoma to white settlement. Section fourteen of the Indian Appropriations Act of 1889 provided for the appointment of a commission to negotiate land cessions with the Cherokee Nation and other tribes owning lands west of the ninety-sixth meridian in Indian Territory. In August 1889, the first formal offers for the sale of the Cherokee Outlet lands were made. By late fall, the white negotiators had formulated a strategy based on the belief that as long as the Cherokees could lease the Outlet for the funds needed to operate their schools and government, the tribe could never be forced to cede the lands. The federal government thus determined to extinguish the Outlet leases in order to coerce the Cherokees into selling those lands.[16]

In 1890 the Oklahoma Organic Act created the Oklahoma Territory from the western half of the old Indian Territory and established a territorial government for the white population. While the Organic Act reduced Indian Territory to the eastern portion of the lands of the Five Tribes and the Quapaw Agency Tribes, it expressly preserved tribal authority and federal Indian jurisdiction in both the Oklahoma and Indian territories. By not including the Cherokee lands and the other tribal domains of the eastern Indian Territory in the new Oklahoma territorial government, Congress was acknowledging treaty guarantees that the lands of the Cherokees and the other Five Tribes would never be subjected to a territorial or state government.

While momentarily honoring the treaty pledge that the Cherokee Nation would never become a part of any state, the federal government coerced the Cherokees into ceding their Outlet lands. On September 19, 1890, President Benjamin Harrison closed the Cherokee Outlet to the cattlemen who had legally leased these grazing lands from the Cherokees. Their validly executed leases were cancelled by executive fiat. Federal troops then occupied the Cherokee Outlet and drove the cattlemen and their herds from the land. Thus, the Cherokees lost the major source of revenue for their school and governmental accounts. Finally, driven to near bankruptcy, the tribe was forced to cede the Outlet land. Years later the Indian Claims Commission found that United States conduct in this transaction had been unconscionable.[17]

Once broken by the Outlet sale, the Cherokees lacked the power and the financial resources to withstand the onslaught of a myriad of congressional enactments. In 1887 the Dawes Act, or General Allotment Act, provided for the transfer of tribal lands to individual Indians. The Cherokees and the other Five Tribes initially escaped the harshness of this first allotment act. During the 1890s the lands of most of the other tribes in the Oklahoma Territory were allotted, pursuant to the General Allotment Act. In 1893 the Dawes Commission was established to seek allotment of the lands of the Five Tribes, and Congress passed the Curtis Act in 1898 to speed up the allotment process. The act provided for the allotment of the Five Tribes' lands and authorized townsites to be opened to non-Indian ownership. A series of allotment agreements and statutes followed. The Five Tribes Act of 1906 addressed allotment and other matters comprehensively. Shortly thereafter, the Oklahoma Enabling Act provided for the admission of Indian Territory and Oklahoma Territory as the single state of Oklahoma.[18]

The final 1906 congressional act, the last in the series originally designed to end the Cherokee government and pave the way for Oklahoma statehood, abruptly reversed the scheme to eliminate the Indian tribe. Instead of eliminating tribal powers, Congress extended them by making a distinction between the Cherokee tribal land base and the Cherokee tribal government. The measure continued indefinitely both tribe and tribal government, preserving both tribal jurisdiction and tribal sovereignty in Oklahoma. Congress had, in the short time since the Curtis and Burke acts and other similar legislation, discovered the utility of retaining a tribal structure. For example, all deeds for Cherokee-allotted lands came from Chief William C. Rogers of the Cherokee tribe and were issued on behalf of the tribe, not the federal government. Thus, land grants to railroads made earlier by Congress without tribal consent never became operative. The Congress had formally recognized the distinctions between tribal landownership and Indian government functions. The terms of the 1906 act for continuing tribal powers are indisputably clear. "Sec. 28. The Tribal existence and present Tribal governments of the Choctaw, Chickasaw, Cherokee, Creek and Seminole Tribes or nations are hereby continued in full force and effect for all purposes authorized by law, until otherwise provided by law."[19]

Ironically, what began as a series of congressional dictates aimed at abolishing tribes and tribal powers, instead specifically retained their power and jurisdiction! No laws have since been enacted to restrict these recognized powers. The Cherokee Nation, even in the face of such coercive and patently illegal action as the cancellation of the Outlet leases, survived.

The tasks of allotment were logistically complex, including creating a tribal membership roll, surveying property, assigning lands, determining contested citizenship, mapping allotments, platting townships, and locating hostile tribal members who refused to enroll in a process they viewed as illegal under treaty guarantees. Every Cherokee had to be located, enrolled, and assigned a piece of land; every piece of land had to be mapped, graded, and assigned. And this had to be done in a hilly country with few roads amid uncooperative, if not hostile, souls. As established by the Dawes Commission, the original final rolls of all political citizens of the Cherokee national government contained 41,889 full-blooded and mixed-blood Cherokees, adopted Delawares and Shawnees, and intermarried whites and freedmen. Tribal land was then divided among these people. Preparation of the rolls began with the Curtis Act in June 1898 and continued through March 1907, with a few additional names being added as late as 1914. The Cherokees did not suffer the Dawes allotment alone. The land base of the Creeks, Choctaws, Seminoles, and Chickasaws was destroyed also. The lands of the Five Tribes at the beginning of the allotment era constituted a total of 19,525,966 acres; 15,794,400 of those acres were allotted to the Indian tribal citizens.[20] The balance of 4 million acres included 309 townsites and segregated coal and timber lands, as well as other allotted lands that were sold at public auction. Seemingly all the Cherokee tribal land was gone. The official Dawes Commission figures indicated that 4,420,068 acres had been allotted among 40,193 enrolled Cherokee.

Even after their land was allotted, the Cherokees entertained one last hope—more symbolic than significant. The twin territories movement was based upon the desire to carve two states out of these territories. The lands of the Five Tribes, known as the Indian Territory, would enter the Union as the state of Sequoyah; the Oklahoma Territory would join the Union as Oklahoma. Cherokees were active in the Sequoyah statehood movement and participated in the Sequoyah Convention held at Muskogee in 1905. The historical governmental experience of the Cherokees and the other Five Tribes was reflected in the Sequoyah Constitution and later in the Oklahoma Constitution. The Sequoyah movement came to naught. In the end, even the hope of a white state with a Cherokee name was too much.[21] Most Cherokees agreed with Will Rogers's bitter epitaph, "We spoiled the best territory in the world to make a state." A white state like Oklahoma was inevitable, Rogers concluded, because "Indians were so cruel they were all killed by civilized white men for encroaching on white domain."[22]

STATEHOOD AND THE STRUGGLE FOR THE
PRESERVATION OF TRIBAL IDENTITY, 1907–46

Statehood and the allotment of tribal lands affected the Cherokees in various ways.[23] Vast numbers who might have been leaders in their little communities or even risen to positions of power in the Cherokee senate or supreme court withdrew from the public arena and retreated back into the hill country. Others, not unlike the Cherokees of old, explored the possibility of migration to Mexico or even to South America. A few, such

as the Cherokee physician and historian Emmet Starr, exiled themselves
to strange places like Saint Louis and Chicago. United States Democratic
Senator Robert L. Owen of Oklahoma captured the national spotlight as
coauthor of the Glass-Owen legislation, which created the Federal Reserve
System. Others became well-known public figures. Will Rogers, of course,
was a great national figure, and Lynn Riggs momentarily gained national
attention when his play about life in the old Cherokee Nation, *Green Grow
the Lilacs,* was transformed into the first of the great modern musicals,
Oklahoma! And, for a brief time during the Second World War, the Cherokee's warrior tradition was alive again in the superb military leadership of
Admiral J. J. (Joco) Clark, a Cherokee born and raised in the prestatehood
Cherokee Nation.[24]

Measured by any objective standard the events of allotment and statehood were a monumental disaster. The desolation of the vast majority of
Cherokees was simply explained by one aging Cherokee farmer speaking
to the Senate policy makers who had brought it about.

Before the allotment scheme was put in effect in the Cherokee Nation
we were a prosperous people. We had farms. Every Indian in this nation
that needed one and felt that he needed it had it. . . . Under our old
Cherokee regime I spent the early days of my life on the farm up here of
300 acres, and arranged to be comfortable in my old age; but the allotment scheme came along and struck me during the crop season. What a
condition! I have 60 acres of land left me; the balance is all gone. I am an
old man, not able to follow the plow as I used to when a boy. What am
I going to do with it? For the last few years, since I have had my allotment, I have gone out there on that farm day after day. I have used the
ax, the hoe, the spade, the plow, hour after hour, til fatigue would throw
me exhausted upon the ground. Next day I repeated the operation, and
let me tell you Senators, I have exerted all my ability, all industry, all
my intelligence if I have any, all my will, all my ambition, the love of
my wife—all those agencies I have employed to make my living out of
that 60 acres, and, God be my Judge, I have not been able to do it. I am
not able to do it. I can't do it. And I am here today, a poor man upon
the verge of starvation—my muscular energy gone, hope gone, I have
nothing to charge my calamity to but the unwise legislation of Congress

in reference to my Cherokee people. . . . I am in that fix. Senators: You will not forget that when I use the word "I" I mean the whole Cherokee people. I am in that fix. What am I to do?[25]

The Dawes Commission's transfer of Indian land had not even been completed when whites began their assault on Indian lands. "It is almost impossible for an allottee," the *Muskogee-Times Democrat* reported, "to get to the office without running the gauntlet of grafters that line the pavements in front of the land office."[26] Grant Foreman, who had been the attorney for the Dawes Commission, estimated that by as early as 1914 not one in ten of the mixed-bloods and freedmen retained any of their original allotment.[27] Kate Barnard, Oklahoma's crusading commissioner of charities and corrections, discovered the theft of the lands of minors and orphans among the Cherokees and other tribes. One report of Barnard's conveys the magnitude of the tragedy. "I have been compelled to see orphans robbed—starved—and buried for money. I have named the men and accused them and furnished the records and affidavits to convict them, but—no result. I decided long ago that Oklahoma had no citizen who cared whether or not an orphan is robbed and starved or killed—because his dead claim is easier to handle than when alive."[28]

Land records in Oklahoma's county courthouses contain thousands of pages documenting the way millions of acres were wrested from the Cherokee. Angie Debo has outlined some of the techniques. "Forgery, embezzlement, criminal conspiracy, misuse of notary's seals, and other crimes against Indian property," she notes, "continued with monotonous regularity."[29]

The 1985 records of the Bureau of Indian Affairs show that fewer than 65,000 acres of the 20 million allotted remain in tribal hands; fewer than a million acres remain in individual Indian hands. By the beginning of the 1930s depression, almost all of the land of the Cherokee was gone. Much of this land was rich with oil, making the land speculator wealthy beyond even his most corrupt dreams. The majority of the Cherokee people, of whom Judge Parker had earlier said, "there is not a pauper Indian amongst them," were now destitute.[30]

By continuing the existence of the tribe in 1906, Congress recognized a crucial reality that the despairing Cherokees themselves had yet come to fully understand. The Cherokee people and their tribal government are separate from the tribal land base. The tribe continued even as their lands were being stolen from them. Tribal sovereignty and tribal jurisdiction survived. The federal government had not needed to abolish the tribe to get the people's land; indeed, in the end, the perpetuation of the tribe was essential to accomplish the tasks of allotment. So while the Cherokee tribe lost its land, its government continued, and soon the sense of being Cherokee—of being the People of Fire—once again emerged. This sustained the Cherokees through the bleak years between the world wars. The traditional Keetoowah Cherokees led by Redbird Smith continued the ancient religious practices, kept alive the primal fires, and nurtured deeper spiritual values. While the Cherokee suffered, somehow the sense of being Cherokee survived amid the most dismal circumstances.

After 1907, the Cherokees' land resources were gone, the treasury depleted, and the formal governmental structure apparently dismantled save for the periodic appointment of a principal chief by the president of the United States. New Deal and other federal and state programs to meet the dire needs of the most destitute of the full-blood families were scant compared to the magnitude of their poverty. Although the legislation was designed to assist them, the Cherokees found little to significantly change their lives in the Oklahoma Indian Welfare Act (1936), coauthored at the height of the depression by United States Congressman William Wirt Hastings, a Cherokee. Due to the woeful lack of tribal organization and significantly diminished congressional appropriations, the overall picture of the Cherokee Nation was indeed bleak.

World War II marked the beginning of change as young tribal members and older Indian leaders were again drawn into the service of the nation. By the mid-1940s Chief Jesse Bartley Milam had brought a skilled hand to tribal organization as well as a renewed sense of pride and possibility. Milam's concern and commitment inspired many Cherokees, including his successor Chief W. W. Keeler, to cooperate with the federal, state, and local governments in seeking solutions to the problems confronting large numbers of Cherokees. The wartime experiences that took thousands of Cherokees beyond the flint hills of eastern Oklahoma, combined with the educational opportunities of the G.I. Bill, brought Cherokees into contact with Indians of other tribes and citizens of other states. The stage was set for change. As World War II came to an end, the Cherokee people stood ready to rebuild both their political and economic tribal life.

RENEWAL OF THE SOVEREIGN CHEROKEE TRIBE, 1946 TO THE PRESENT

The Indian Claims Commission (1946) provided the opportunity for the tribe to capitalize upon a renewed sense of Cherokee spirit. The commission, designed to provide a forum for the litigation of Indian claims against the United States, drew the Cherokees together around a common purpose. Ultimately, the tribe brought itself under the organizational umbrella of the Oklahoma Indian Welfare Act, and special legislation formally reaffirmed their status as the Cherokee tribe of Oklahoma. Thus the Cherokees began the task of litigating their historic claims. The old joke heard for almost half a century, among full bloods, "I'll pay you when I get my claims money," was about to become a serious possibility. The tribe hired legal counsel, including the indomitable Earl Boyd Pierce and the scholarly Paul Neibell, and went about the task of re-creating a tribal structure capable of managing the tasks ahead.[31]

The Indian Claims Commission found that the Cherokee Nation, against their will and for an unconscionable consideration, had been forced to deed to the government 6,022,000 acres of their fee-title land, known as the Cherokee Outlet, in northwestern Oklahoma. This land had been the object of the Oklahoma run in 1893 when 40,000 United States citizens were given free homesteads of 160 acres each. In 1902, the 41,000 Cherokee citizens received only 100 acres each, including the barren flint hills where many full bloods lived and remain today.

The Claims Commission awarded the Cherokee Nation nearly $19 million without interest as a judgment payment for the Outlet lands. In 1962, Congress directed per capita payments to be made from this judgment to all persons, or their legal heirs, whose names appeared upon the rolls prepared by the Dawes Commission and by statute on March 4, 1907. More than 80,000 individuals received small individual payments. The Distribution Act of 1962 also provided that any unclaimed funds not allocated per capita should revert to the Cherokee Nation and be "advanced and expended" by the principal chief with the approval of the secretary of the interior. These unallocated funds provided the seed money for the economic rebirth of the Cherokee tribe.

After the Outlet case the Cherokee Nation turned to the resolution of another injustice, known popularly as the Riverbed case. Under the original Cherokee patent of 1835 the tribe had been given fee title to the land, including the waterways, within the Indian Territory. The Cherokee general counsel, Earl Boyd Pierce, made a futile effort to negotiate with the state of Oklahoma the question of title and royalties due the tribe from sand, gravel, and gas production from the Arkansas River. Upon discovering that the Interior and Justice departments would assume a neutral attitude, the Cherokee attorneys, Pierce and Andrew C. Wilcoxen, entered suit in December 1966. The attorneys asserted that all of the riverbed above the mouth of the Canadian River to Muskogee and the northern half below the Canadian River to the Arkansas state line belonged to the Cherokee Nation. They argued that the United States could neither have reserved the Arkansas riverbed nor have transferred Cherokee land to the state of Oklahoma. The tribal suit sought not only an accounting against the state of Oklahoma, sixteen oil companies, and two sand and gravel companies, but also an injunction against interference with Cherokee possession of the property. The state had, in fact, collected a total of about $8 million for the riverbed reserves. The Choctaw and Chickasaw nations intervened in the Cherokee suit in the summer of 1967 and became parties to the judgment.

After adverse decisions by the federal District Court at Muskogee and the United States Court of Appeals at Denver, the landmark case reached the United States Supreme Court. The attorneys for the Interior and Justice departments eventually joined the Indian nations in the litigation, preparing amicus briefs on behalf of the tribes. In 1970, the high court finally ruled in a classic four-to-three decision. The Supreme Court found that the 100-mile stretch of the navigable portion of the Arkansas River from Fort Smith, Arkansas, up to Muskogee, Oklahoma, belonged to the Cherokee, the Choctaw, and Chickasaw nations. To this day the Cherokee claim against the United States is yet unpaid. A Corps of Engineers study mandated by Congress has found the value of the resources illegally taken to be almost $150 million. This is money desperately needed by the Cherokee people, and yet Congress, which must appropriate the money, has chosen not to act. The state of Oklahoma promptly repaid the tribe the $8 million they had collected from riverbed resources.[32]

The earlier Outlet judgment provided the tribal resources necessary for the revitalization of the Cherokee Nation. The Riverbed judgment would help finish the task. Chief Milam and his successor, W. W. Keeler, provided initial leadership from the 1940s to the 1970s for this revitalization. Chief Keeler was the most powerful, enigmatic, and controversial Cherokee tribal leader since John Ross. As president and chief executive officer of Phillips Petroleum, Keeler had a significant national power base. He knew how to manipulate the federal structure, and the tribe benefited mightily from his power and position. Nonetheless, many felt he failed to understand the needs of traditional and full-blood Cherokees. Although considerable hostility and agitation marked his final years, there is no question that when Keeler retired as chief, the Cherokee Nation had become a vital force once again.

Under Keeler's leadership and the leadership of his successors, Ross Swimmer and Wilma Mankiller, the Cherokees have established major programs for business enterprise and tribal employment. They have repurchased tribal lands, written and adopted a new constitution, and exerted renewed influence within the state of Oklahoma and the United States. In the early days of the Reagan administration Chief Swimmer headed the Presidential Commission on Indian Reservation Economies and was later named to the highest position on native policy as undersecretary of the interior for Indian affairs. Beginning with Keeler's chieftainship, the tribe drew upon New Frontier and Great Society programs to provide a base for individual tribal development while calling upon the private sector to build self-sustaining sources of employment for tribal members. Symbolic of these efforts is the Cherokee tribal complex outside of Tahlequah, with the Cherokee Nation building, greenhouses, child-care centers, and offices owned by the tribe and rented to the Bureau of Indian Affairs, as well as the Cultural Center at nearby Park Hill, which includes an ancient village, a major outdoor theater, a museum, and a reconstructed nineteenth-century tribal village.

Without question the most significant recent achievement of the Cherokees was the return of popular sovereignty. From statehood until 1970, the principal chief of the Cherokees had been appointed by the president of the United States without advice, consent, or ballot of the Cherokees themselves. In 1970 the popular election of Chief Keeler, who had been previously named by every president from Harry Truman to Richard Nixon, brought an end to the era of colonial appointment of Cherokee tribal leadership. Other recognitions of inherent judicial and legal sovereignty have quickly followed. Today the Cherokees stand on an equal footing with other tribes and state governments as the sovereign entities described by John Marshall in *Cherokee Nation v. Georgia* and *Worcester v. Georgia*. When provided with an opportunity to claim portions of this jurisdiction over the Indians by Public Law 280, the state of Oklahoma chose not to pursue this option. Today such a claim would be precluded without tribal consent by provisions of the Indian Civil Rights Act. Thus, the Cherokee tribe survives as a sovereign governmental force ready to address the needs of her people.

The Cherokee tribe is in the midst of a major cultural revival. Arts and crafts are once again being encouraged; the Cherokee language is spoken by 15,000 to 25,000 tribal members, and a strong bilingual program keeps the language alive among the youngest Cherokees. IBM has created a typewriter-script ball in the Sequoyahan syllabary, and King Features has even issued comics in the Cherokee language. The Sequoyah Medallion, presented first to the inventor of the syllabary, has been restruck and awarded to Cherokee linguists Jack and Anna Kilpatrick for their scholarship and to the artist Cecil Dick for his long career as a distinguished painter. At the same time, the traditional Keetoowahs continue to celebrate on July 19 with the reading of the ancient and sacred wampum belts and the renewal of the fire. The tribe has come a long way in throwing off the popular image created by the Indian humorist who joked that all Cherokees were descendants of white princesses. In truth, the traditional Cherokee is a stronger and more powerful influence in tribal affairs than at any time since removal.

As they prepared to enter the twenty-first century, the tribe has acted very Cherokee. In 1976, reaffirming what they have so often done in days of transition, the tribe adopted a new constitution. The nation called a constitutional convention, revised their old governance documents in light of new circumstances, and submitted it to popular referendum. Approved by a tribal vote of about ten to one, the Cherokee Constitution symbolizes, once again, faith in law as an instrument of survival. One hopes that this time the tribe's faith will not be betrayed as it has been over the past three centuries.

When Chief Ross Swimmer was called to Washington by President Ronald Reagan to head the Bureau of Indian Affairs, the elected assistant principal chief, Wilma Mankiller, came to office. Thus she became the first woman to serve as chief of the Cherokee Nation, bringing forward and fulfilling a tradition of leadership that dates back to the "Beloved Women" leaders of the precontact and preconstitutional eras. In the summer of 1987, Wilma Mankiller was elected principal chief. Speaking of her electoral victory, Mankiller said that the most important thing about her election was not that she was a woman but that she represented a different kind of Cherokee, from a new background, with a different agenda. She did not have a national power base, profession, or position of wealth, but rather she was an Indian from an Indian community who had worked with Indian needs within the Indian nation. Mankiller had earlier come to prominence in connection with the Bell Project, a self-help program to bring water to the people of a back hills community. Her election suggests that the Cherokees are once again looking inward, using and building their greatest resource, the Cherokee people themselves.

The path ahead for Chief Mankiller, her people, and their descendants will probably be no smoother than the path of Raven Mocker, John Ross, Major Ridge, and their Cherokee ancestors. Poverty still blights the flint hills of the full bloods. Crime, unemployment, alcoholism, and drugs are no strangers to the Cherokees. Modern Cherokees continue to be subject to forces as diverse as health-care workers who sterilize Indian women without their consent and the nation's elected leaders, who in the name of national budget cutting refuse to pay the Riverbed judgment, while appropriating billions for aid to foreign governments.[33]

Increasingly, Cherokees are taking control of their own fate and becoming less dependent upon federal and state actions. They are once again a people with a sense of control of their own destinies. The values that survive are at the heart of the Cherokee's historic tribal existence—among these are family, friends, and a sense of being a people with a place and a mission. This spirit of survival is reflected in the observations of a Cherokee tribesman.

Cherokees have changed since I was a boy. Almost everyone has a car and they have started building government houses for the Cherokees. A lot of men and women work in town and have regular jobs at plants or on farms. But the Little People still live in the caves and protect Cherokees. My people have not really changed inside. Boys still play at hunting buffalo and English is still a struggle at school. In the spring Cherokees pick strawberries and eat the wild foods. And every summer the people come back and dance at the fires. Being an Indian, being a Cherokee, doesn't depend upon how you dress or whether you have an old Ford or a young pony. Being a Cherokee is a way of thinking and a way of knowing. The Cherokees in bright cars and neat suits are still men of the eagle race, the people of the eternal fire. And we are still a proud people who have kept alive a great spirit. The eternal fire still burns brightly for my people, the Cherokees.[34]

NOTES

1. James McClellan, *Joseph Story and the American Constitution,* 299 n. 115; *Worcester v. Georgia,* 31 U.S. 6 Pet. 515 (1832).

2. The single most revealing portrait of the survival of the Cherokee and their culture is a bilingual booklet entitled *The Cherokee People Today: A Report to the Cherokee People,* compiled by Albert L. Wahrhaftig and translated by Calvin Nackedhead, with drawings by Donald Vann (Tahlequah: Carnegie Cross-Cultural Education Project, 1966). The report indicates that more Cherokees than ever before are participating in community activities and that the number of Cherokee speakers has grown. Not so surprising was the finding that the Cherokees are poor, with incomes about half those of whites. A similar study today would conclude, as this one did, that the one thing that helps Cherokees "get along" is the Cherokee community itself. For a brief general overview of Cherokee history, including the modern era, see Theda Perdue, *The Cherokee* (New York: Chelsea House Publishers, 1989); Earl Boyd Pierce and Rennard Strickland, *The Cherokee People* (Phoenix: Indian Tribal Series, 1973); and Rennard Strickland, *The Indians in Oklahoma* (Norman: University of Oklahoma Press, 1980).

3. The conflict from the perspective of the treaty party is outlined in Thurman Wilkins, *Cherokee Tragedy: The Story of the Ridge Family and the Decimation of a People* (New York: Macmillan, 1970), and from the Ross viewpoint in Gary E. Moulton, *John Ross: Cherokee Chief* (Athens: University of Georgia Press, 1978). See particu-

larly Gerard Reed, "Postremoval Factionalism in the Cherokee Nation," in *The Cherokee Indian Nation: A Troubled History*, ed. Duane King (Knoxville: University of Tennessee Press, 1979), and Gary E. Moulton, "Chief John Ross and the Internal Crisis of the Cherokee Nation," in *Indian Leaders: Oklahoma's First Statesmen*, ed. H. Glenn Jordan and Thomas M. Holms (Oklahoma City: Oklahoma Historical Society, 1979).

4. The crisis of the legal system and the politicalization of the courts can be seen in Grant Foreman, ed., *Indian Justice* (Oklahoma City: Harlow, 1934). The analysis and response of Cherokee partisan John Rollin Ridge can be found in David Farmer and Rennard Strickland, *A Trumpet of Our Own: Yellow Bird on the American Indian* (San Francisco: Book Club of California, 1981).

5. Samuel Worcester, Worcester-Robertson Papers, McFarlin Library, University of Tulsa, Tulsa, Okla. (reprinted in Pierce and Strickland, *Cherokee People*, 34). The literature on black slavery often provides the best picture of the stratified groups within Cherokee society. See, for example, Theda Perdue, *Slavery and the Evolution of Cherokee Society, 1540–1866* (Knoxville: University of Tennessee Press, 1979), and Richard Halliburton, Jr., *Red Over Black: Black Slavery Among the Cherokees* (Westport, Conn.: Greenwood Press, 1977).

6. The major work on Cherokees during the Civil War era remains Annie H. Abel's monumental three-volume study, *The American Indian as Slaveholder and Secessionist; The American Indian as Participant in the Civil War;* and *The American Indian Under Reconstruction* (Cleveland: Arthur H. Clarke, 1915, 1919, 1925). See also Kenny A. Franks, *Stand Watie and the Agony of the Cherokee Nation* (Memphis: Memphis State University Press, 1979); LeRoy H. Fisher, ed., *The Civil War Era in Indian Territory* (Los Angeles: L. L. Morrison, 1974); Lary G. Rampp and Donald L. Rampp, *The Civil War in the Indian Territory* (Austin: Presidial Press, 1975); Angie Debo, "Southern Refugees of the Cherokee Nation," *Southwestern Historical Quarterly* 35 (1932): 255–66.

7. The most recent book on the Cherokees who fought at Pea Ridge is W. Craig Gaines, *The Confederate Cherokees: John Drew's Regiment of Mounted Rifles* (Baton Rouge: Louisiana State University Press, 1989).

8. The most touching account of the devastation of the war and the horrors of Reconstruction is in the family letters collected by Edward E. Dale and Gaston Litton, eds., *Cherokee Cavaliers: Forty Years of Cherokee History as Told in the Correspondence of the Ridge-Watie-Boudinot Family* (Norman: University of Oklahoma Press, 1939). The documents of Reconstruction are gathered in Abel, *American Indian Under Reconstruction*. A more recent account is Bailey M. Thomas, *Reconstruction in Indian Territory: A Story of Avarice, Discrimination, and Opportunism* (Port Washington, N.Y.: Kennikat Press, 1972). Wiley Britton's early work remains

particularly enlightening; see "Some Reminiscences of the Cherokee People Returning to Their Homes: The Exiles of a Nation," *Chronicles of Oklahoma* 6 (1928): 163–77.

9. Much of the following analysis is suggested by H. Craig Miner in *The Corporation and the Indian: Tribal Sovereignty and Industrial Civilization in Indian Territory, 1865–1907* (Columbia: University of Missouri Press, 1976). The story of the coming of the railroad is vividly told in V. V. Masterson, *The Katy Railroad and the Last Frontier* (Norman: University of Oklahoma Press, 1952).

10. *Protest of the Cherokee Nation Against a Territorial Government,* January 30, 1871, 9, micropublished in "Western Americana," reel 105. The authors are indebted to Margaret Shanks Guffey for the location of most of the materials cited on the Cherokee protest movement. This analysis draws heavily upon her excellent master's thesis, "Wresting Land from Indian Hands: The Indian Response to Land Transfers" (University of Tulsa, 1983).

11. *Remonstrance of the Cherokee, Creek, Choctaw, and Seminole Delegations,* February 28, 1876, 3–4, Lester Hargett Collection, Thomas Gilcrease Institute, Tulsa, Okla.

12. For the most complete analysis of internal politics, see Morris L. Wardell, *A Political History of the Cherokee Nation, 1803–1907* (Norman: University of Oklahoma Press, 1938).

13. The papers and speeches of the Ross heir are gathered in Mrs. William Potter Ross, ed., *The Life and Times of Hon. William P. Ross* (Fort Smith, Ark.: Privately printed, 1893). The best recent research on Boudinot is Thomas Burnell Colbert, "Prophet of Progress: The Life and Times of Elias Cornelius Boudinot" (Ph.D. diss., Oklahoma State University, 1982).

14. Speaking before one of the seemingly endless congressional hearings on conditions among the Cherokees, Isaac C. Parker, United States district judge for the Western District of Arkansas and the Indian Territory, declared that there was "not a pauper Indian amongst them." I. C. Parker, Cherokee Materials, Shleppey Collection, McFarlin Library, University of Tulsa. A standard work on Parker is the popular turn-of-the-century account *Hell on the Border: He Hanged Them High,* ed. Rennard Strickland and Jack Gregory (Muskogee, Okla.: Indian Heritage Association, 1971). A portion of Parker's congressional testimony is included in an appendix to that edition.

15. Judge Parker testified in Congress that "there has been a contest between savageness and civilization. The savageness is not upon the part of the Indians but . . . by the refugee criminal classes who have obtruded themselves upon that people from every State in the Union, and who have been doing it from the day the Treaty of Hopewell was entered into to this very hour." Testimony, January 10, 1895,

House Committee on the Judiciary, reprinted in Strickland and Gregory, eds., *Hell on the Border*, 195–99. For a more detailed discussion, see Rennard Strickland, *Fire and the Spirits: Cherokee Law from Clan to Court* (Norman: University of Oklahoma Press, 1975). The exciting story of law and lawlessness is found in the following: Homer Croy, *He Hanged Them High: An Authentic Account of the Hanged Eighty-Eight Men* (New York: Duell, Sloan and Pearce, 1952); Fred Harvey Harrington, *Hanging Judge* (Caldwell, Idaho: Caxton Printers, 1951); C. H. McKennon, *Iron Men: A Saga of the Deputy United States Marshals Who Rode the Indian Territory* (Garden City, N.Y.: Doubleday, 1967); Glenn Shirley, *Law West of Fort Smith: A History of Frontier Justice in Indian Territory, 1834–1896* (New York: Henry Holt, 1957).

16. *Proceedings*, Councils between the U.S. Commissioners and the Cherokee Nation, December 3–26, 1890, November 18–19, 1891, testimony of December 17, 1890, 176, Earl Boyd Pierce Papers, Cherokee Archives, Talequah (copy in Shleppey Collection, McFarlin Library, University of Tulsa). See also Berlin B. Chapman, "Opening of the Cherokee Outlet: An Archival Study," *Chronicles of Oklahoma* 40 (1962): 158–81, 253–85.

17. At the time, Cherokee delegate Lucien Bell bitterly denounced the federal action. "This land that we hold here is not a gift on the part of the United States, it is not a charity arrangement at all, it has been paid for four times over . . . ; we gave up a country in the civilized part of the United States and took for it this wilderness." Chapman, "Opening of the Cherokee Outlet, 187."

18. For the complete text of all acts, see *Laws Relating to the Five Civilized Tribes in Oklahoma, 1890–1914* (Washington, D.C.: Government Printing Office, 1915). See also Felix Cohen, *Handbook of Federal Indian Law* (Charlottesville, Va.: Michie, 1982), 779–80, 782–88. For an insightful analysis of the step-by-step development of this law, see F. Browning Pipestem, "The Mythology of the Oklahoma Indians Revisited: A Survey of the Legal Status of Indian Tribes in Oklahoma Eleven Years Later," in *Sovereignty Symposium II: Divergent Points of View* (Oklahoma City: Papers of the Oklahoma Supreme Court Conference, 1989). For a comparative understanding, see Pipestem's earlier article, "The Journey from *Ex Parte Crow Dog* to *Littlechief*: A Survey of Tribal and Criminal Jurisdiction in Western Oklahoma," *American Indian Law Review* 6 (1978): 1–80, and Susan Work, "The 'Terminated' Five Tribes of Oklahoma: The Effect of Federal Legislation and Administrative Treatment on the Government of the Seminole Nation," *American Indian Law Review* 6 (1978): 81–141.

19. "An Act to Provide for the Final Disposition of the Affairs of the Five Civilized Tribes in the Indian Territory," April 26, 1906, ch. 1876, 34 Stat. 137 (1906).

20. The original allotment records and cards for enrollment are maintained by the Bureau of Indian Affairs at the Muskogee Area Office. This material is drawn from an examination of those documents. The definitive history of the Dawes

Commission in Oklahoma has yet to be written. For a general overview of Dawes, see Wilcomb E. Washburn, ed., *The Assault on Indian Tribalism: The General Allotment Law (Dawes Act) of 1887* (Philadelphia: J. B. Lippincott, 1975), and D. S. Otis, *The Dawes Act and the Allotment of Indian Lands,* ed. Francis Paul Prucha (Norman: University of Oklahoma Press, 1973).

21. See, generally, Amos Maxwell, *The Sequoyah Convention* (Boston: Meador Publishing, 1953), and Rennard Strickland and James C. Thomas, "Most Sensibly Conservative and Safely Radical: Oklahoma's Constitutional Regulation of Economic Power, Land Ownership, and Corporate Monopoly," *Tulsa Law Review* 9 (1973): 67–238.

22. Richard M. Ketchum, *Will Rogers: His Life and Times* (New York: Simon and Schuster, 1975), 51; "Will Rogers," Typescript, Shleppey Collection, McFarlin Library, University of Tulsa.

23. Few whites ever understood the emotional depth of the Indians' agony at the passing of their nationhood. Edward Everett Dale wrote with some surprise of the sadness an Indian woman felt when she remembered the 1907 festivities to celebrate Oklahoma statehood. The Cherokee woman refused to attend the statehood ceremonies with her white husband. He returned and said to her: "Well, Mary, we no longer live in the Cherokee Nation. All of us are now citizens of the state of Oklahoma." Tears came to her eyes as thirty years later she recalled that day. "It broke my heart. I went to bed and cried all night long. It seemed more than I could bear that the Cherokee Nation, my country and my people's country was no more." Edward Everett Dale, "Two Mississippi Valley Frontiers," *Chronicles of Oklahoma* 26 (Winter 1948–49): 382.

24. For examples of the varied lives of selected twentieth-century Cherokees, see Rennard Strickland and Jack Gregory, "Emmet Starr, Heroic Historian: 1870–1930," in *American Indian Intellectuals,* ed. Margot Liberty (Saint Paul: West Publishing, 1978), 105–14; Phyllis Cole Braunlich, *Haunted by Home: The Life and Letters of Lynn Riggs* (Norman: University of Oklahoma Press, 1988); Ketchum, *Will Rogers;* Robert J. Conley, *The Witch of Goingsnake and Other Stories* (Norman: University of Oklahoma Press, 1988); and the brief biographical sketches in the appendix to Pierce and Strickland, *Cherokee People.*

25. D. W. C. Duncan, "Conditions in the Indian Territory," in *Great Documents in American History,* ed. Wayne Moquin (New York: Praeger Publishers, 1973), 286–89.

26. *Muskogee-Times Democrat,* May 1, 1906.

27. Grant Foreman, "Protecting the Indian," *The Independent* (New York), January 2, 1913, 39–42.

28. *Muskogee-Times Democrat,* May 10, 1910.

29. Angie Debo, *And Still the Waters Run: The Betrayal of the Five Civilized*

Tribes (Princeton: Princeton University Press, 1940), 312. Debo's book is a definitive analysis, which exposes the graft and corruption with such accuracy that it has been regularly cited by courts of law in sustaining contemporary Indian rights.

30. Surveys by the Indian Rights Association contain the most disturbing but accurate accounts of the Cherokees and other Oklahoma Indians during the period of allotment. Angie Debo prepared such a survey, which was published as *The Five Civilized Tribes of Oklahoma: Report on Social and Economic Conditions* (Philadelphia: Indian Rights Association, 1951). Another helpful work is B. T. Quinten, "Oklahoma Tribes, the Great Depression, and the Indian Bureau," *Mid-America* 49 (1967): 29–43. The Indian and Pioneer Papers Project interviewed Cherokees during the depression era, and these oral histories are available at the Oklahoma Historical Society and in the Western History Collection at the University of Oklahoma. See also Theda Perdue, *Nations Remembered: An Oral History of the Five Civilized Tribes, 1865–1907* (Westport, Conn.: Greenwood Press, 1980).

31. Earl Boyd Pierce's personal account of the Outlet and Riverbed litigation and its subsequent impact is found in Pierce and Strickland, *Cherokee People,* 62–73. Official records, exhibits, dockets, and other documents can be found in the Indian Claims Commission Papers, McFarlin Library, University of Tulsa. All of Pierce's papers were left to the Cherokee Historical Society at Tahlequah. The Riverbed case is still before the courts under the direction of James G. Wilcoxen, who is the general counsel of the Cherokee Nation of Oklahoma and the son of one of the lawyers who originally filed the case on behalf of the tribe.

32. Pierce and Strickland, *Cherokee People,* 62–73.

33. The material gathered by the Carnegie Cross-Cultural Education Project of the University of Chicago provides the most complete picture of the challenges facing the contemporary Cherokee and the traditional community. In recent years the tribe has begun to accumulate similar data and is now the primary source to which those interested may turn. The following sources are recommended: Albert L. Wahrhaftig and Robert K. Thomas, "Renaissance and Repression: The Oklahoma Cherokee," *Trans-Action* 6 (1969): 42–48; Wahrhaftig, "The Tribal Cherokee Population of Eastern Oklahoma," *Current Anthropology* 9 (1968): 510–18; Wahrhaftig, "Institution Building Among Oklahoma's Traditional Cherokees," in *Four Centuries of Southern Indians,* ed. Charles M. Hudson (Athens: University of Georgia Press, 1975), 132–47; and Wahrhaftig and Jane Lukens-Wahrhaftig, "New Militants or Resurrected State? The Five County Northeastern Oklahoma Cherokee Organization," in *Cherokee Nation,* ed. King, 223–46.

34. Jack Gregory and Rennard Strickland, *Adventures of an Indian Boy* (Muskogee, Okla.: Indian Heritage Association, 1972), 29.

Bibliographical Essay

WILLIAM L. ANDERSON

Without a doubt the Cherokee Indians have played one of the most significant roles in American history. Perhaps rightfully, then, more has been written about those native Americans than about almost any other Indian tribe. This essay attempts to briefly cite valuable works of the prehistoric and colonial periods, with the major focus on removal and the period immediately preceding it. For a more detailed bibliography and a listing of the sources and their locations, readers should consult Francis Paul Prucha's works: *A Bibliographic Guide to the History of Indian-White Relations in the United States* (Chicago: University of Chicago Press, 1977), and *Indian-White Relations in the United States: A Bibliography of Works Published, 1975–1980* (Lincoln: University of Nebraska Press, 1978). Over a decade ago Raymond D. Fogelson compiled for the Newberry Library an extremely useful book entitled *The Cherokees: A Critical Bibliography* (Bloomington: Indiana University Press, 1978). For a listing of documents and their locations one might consult William L. Anderson and James A. Lewis, *A Guide to Cherokee Documents in Foreign Archives* (Metuchen, N.J.: Scarecrow Press, 1983), and Paul Kutsche, *A Guide to Cherokee Documents in the Northeastern United States* (Metuchen, N.J.: Scarecrow Press, 1986). The Anderson and Lewis guide lists almost ten thousand documents from England, France, Spain, Mexico, and Canada, which are all available on interlibrary loan from Western Carolina University in Cullowhee, N.C.

A delightful beginning point for studying Cherokee history or any native American group can be found in James Axtell, "The Indian in American History," in *Occasional Papers in Curriculum Series* 2 (Chicago: The Newberry Library, 1985): 1–30. Axtell speculates on what American history might have been like had there been no native Americans when the Europeans arrived.

PREHISTORIC

For an understanding of the most recent thought on Cherokee prehistoric origins, one should consult Joffre Coe, "Cherokee Archaeology," in *Symposium on Cherokee and Iroquois Culture*, ed. William N. Fenton and John Gulick, Smithsonian Institution, Bureau of American Ethnology Bulletin no. 180 (Washington, D.C.: Government Printing Office, 1961); Roy S. Dickens, *Cherokee Prehistory: The Pisgah Phase in the Appalachian Summit Region* (Knoxville: University of Tennessee Press, 1976); and Bennie C. Keel, *Cherokee Archaeology: A Study of the Appalachian Summit* (Knoxville: University of Tennessee Press, 1976). The Dickens and Keel books deal mainly with North Carolina sites. For sites elsewhere, primarily in Tennessee, see Jefferson Chapman, *Tellico Archaeology: Twelve Thousand Years of Native American History*, University of Tennessee, Department of Anthropology, Publication no. 43 (Knoxville: University of Tennessee Press, 1985), and Gerald F. Schroedl, *Overhill Cherokee Archaeology at Chota-Tennessee*, University of Tennessee, Department of Anthropology, Publication no. 38 (Knoxville: University of Tennessee Press, 1986). Dated but still useful is Cyrus Thomas, *Cherokee in Pre-Columbian Times* (New York: Hodges, 1890).

COLONIAL

To get a feeling for Cherokee culture, one should look at James Mooney's "Myths of the Cherokees," Bureau of American Ethnology, *Nineteenth Annual Report, 1897–98*, pt. 1 (Washington, D.C.: Government Printing Office, 1900). Although written at the turn of the century, Mooney's work contains much useful information as well as a brief history of the Cherokee. The best modern synthesis of Indian culture and one that contains a great deal on the Cherokee is Charles Hudson, *The Southeastern Indians* (Knoxville: University of Tennessee Press, 1977).

Bibliographical Essay

Surveys of Cherokee history prior to removal can be found in John P. Brown, *Old Frontiers: The Story of the Cherokee Indians from Earliest Times to the Date of Removal* (Kingsport, Tenn.: Southern Publishers, 1938; reprint, New York: Arno Press, 1971), and in Grace Steele Woodward, *The Cherokees* (Norman: University of Oklahoma Press, 1963). Woodward's history covers the period to 1907, when Oklahoma became a state, while Marion L. Starkey, *The Cherokee Nation* (New York: Alfred A. Knopf, 1946; reprint, New York: Russell and Russell, 1972), is especially strong for the immediate pre-removal period. John P. Reid, *A Better Kind of Hatchet: Law, Trade, and Diplomacy in the Cherokee Nation During the Early Years of European Contact* (University Park, Penn.: Pennsylvania State University Press, 1976), is essential in understanding the impact and destructiveness of European trade and contact on the Indians. How Cherokee law and society dealt with the white man is revealed in the works of two legal historians, John P. Reid, *A Law of Blood: The Primitive Law of the Cherokee Nation* (New York: New York University Press, 1970), and Rennard Strickland, *Fire and the Spirits: Cherokee Law from Clan to Court* (Norman: University of Oklahoma Press, 1975). Reid's *Law of Blood* is also an excellent study of the Cherokee kinship system. Frederick O. Gearing, *Priests and Warriors: Social Structures for Cherokee Politics in the Eighteenth Century* (Menasha, Wis.: American Anthropological Association, 1962), describes the Cherokee political system, while Gary C. Goodwin, *Cherokees in Transition: A Study of Changing Culture and Environment Prior to 1775* (Chicago: University of Chicago, Department of Geography, 1977), is a good examination of the relationship between Cherokee culture and environment.

One of the most valuable printed sources on eighteenth-century Cherokees is James Adair, *History of the American Indians,* ed. Samuel Cole Williams (1775; Johnson City, Tenn.: Watauga Press, 1930). Adair was a trader for more than thirty years with the Cherokee and the Chickasaw. Although Adair was an evangelist for the idea that the Indians descended from the Ten Lost Tribes of Israel, his valuable insights into Cherokee life, culture, and politics make this work indispensable. Another valuable firsthand account is the recordings of Lt. Henry Timberlake in *Memoirs, 1756–1765,* ed. Samuel Cole Williams (1765; reprint, Johnson City, Tenn.: Watauga Press, 1927). Timberlake was a soldier who lived among the Cherokee for several months after the French and Indian War. He later escorted two groups of Cherokees to London. Adair's and Timberlake's editor, Samuel

Cole Williams, also compiled a useful collection of observations on the Cherokees in *Early Travels in the Tennessee Country, 1540–1800* (Johnson City, Tenn.: Watauga Press, 1928). Included in *Early Travels* is the journal of the Scottish nobleman Sir Alexander Cuming, who visited the Cherokees in 1730 and persuaded seven of them to return to England with him. William Bartram, the noted naturalist, also turned his keen power of observation on the Cherokees. Francis Harper's edition of Bartram's adventures adds significantly to the identification and location of many otherwise obscure Cherokees, traders, and places in *The Travels of William Bartram: Naturalist's Edition*, ed. Francis Harper (New Haven: Yale University Press, 1958).

The period from 1740 to 1762 is admirably treated in David H. Corkran, *Cherokee Frontier: Conflict and Survival* (Norman: University of Oklahoma Press, 1962). James O'Donnell III has perhaps the best work on the Indian involvement in the American Revolution in his *Southern Indians in the American Revolution* (Knoxville: University of Tennessee Press, 1973). He has also written a briefer, more focused account of the Cherokee activity, *The Cherokees of North Carolina in the American Revolution* (Raleigh: North Carolina Division of Archives and History, Department of Cultural Resources, 1976). In addition to describing the specific activities of the Cherokees during the Revolution, O'Donnell points out that the Cherokees and other southern Indians really had no choice in fighting for the British. Perhaps the Cherokees' most significant impact in this fray was their early devastating defeat, a setback that made other tribes hesitate to take more than a limited part in the war.

FEDERAL

The federal period saw the development of governmental programs to civilize the Indians. In many ways the Cherokees served as a model for those who argued that such an approach was appropriate and even possible. The tremendous advances by the Cherokees during this period in developing a written constitution, political institutions based on those of the United States, and a written language and press are covered quite satisfactorily in Henry T. Malone, *Cherokees of the Old South: A People in Transition* (Athens: University of Georgia Press, 1956), and in Mary Young, "The Cherokee Nation: Mirror of the Republic," *American Quarterly* 33 (Winter 1981):

502–23. See also William G. McLoughlin, "Experiment in Cherokee Citizenship, 1817–1829," *American Quarterly* 33 (Spring 1981): 3–25. Maj. John Norton, a Cherokee raised by the Mohawks who visited the Cherokees in 1816, recorded much geographic and ethnographic information, which may be found in *The Journal of Major John Norton, 1816,* ed. Carl F. Klinck and James J. Talman (Toronto: Publications of the Champlain Society, 1970). William G. McLoughlin has collected many of his articles on Cherokee nationalism, slavery, and missionaries in a volume entitled *The Cherokee Ghost Dance and Other Essays on the Southeastern Indians* (Macon, Ga.: Mercer University Press, 1984). McLoughlin has also published a political narrative covering roughly the same period as Henry Malone's work, but more from the point of view of the Cherokees, *Cherokee Renascence in the New Republic* (Princeton: Princeton University Press, 1986). For a good brief description, see Richard S. Persico, "Early Nineteenth Century Political Organizations," in *The Cherokee Indian Nation: A Troubled History,* ed. Duane H. King (Knoxville: University of Tennessee Press, 1979), 92–109. For maps and details of the background to the various treaties involving the numerous land cessions concerning the Cherokees, one should consult Charles C. Royce, *The Cherokee Nation of Indians* (reprint, Chicago: Aldine Publishing, 1975).

The part played by the missionaries (Moravian, Presbyterian, Congregationalist, Baptist, and Methodist) in proselytizing, civilizing, and removal is covered by William G. McLoughlin's *Cherokees and Missionaries, 1789–1839* (New Haven: Yale University Press, 1984). By using new sources and emphasizing primary materials, McLoughlin does an excellent job of describing the complexities and inconsistencies of both Cherokee-White relations and inter-tribal relations. McLoughlin's is the most thorough work on the missionaries, but Robert S. Walker, *Torchlight to the Cherokees: The Brainerd Mission* (New York: Macmillan, 1931), is still valuable for its treatment of the famous Cherokee missionary school. One noted missionary to the Cherokees with whom almost everyone is acquainted through his involvement with the Supreme Court case (*Worcester v. Georgia*) is Samuel Worcester, subject of Althea Bass's biography, *Cherokee Messenger* (Norman: University of Oklahoma Press, 1936). William McLoughlin has completed a dual biography of two missionaries who were with the Cherokees before and after removal, *Champions of the Cherokees: Evan and*

John Jones (Princeton: Princeton University Press, 1989). Brief scholarly accounts of other missionaries among the Cherokees may be found in: Dorothy C. Bass, "Gideon Blackburn's Mission to the Cherokees," *Journal of Presbyterian History* 52 (Fall 1974): 203–26; Henry T. Malone, "The Early Nineteenth Century Missionaries in the Cherokee Country," *Tennessee Historical Quarterly* 10 (June 1951): 127–139; James W. Moffitt, "Early Baptist Missionary Work Among the Cherokees," *East Tennessee Historical Society Publications*, no. 12 (1940): 16–27; Mary T. Peacock, "Methodist Mission Work Among the Cherokees Before Removal," *Methodist History* 3 (April 1965): 20–39.

Theda Perdue describes the role of black slavery in the Cherokee Nation in *Slavery and the Evolution of Cherokee Society, 1540–1866* (Knoxville: University of Tennessee Press, 1979). Perdue maintains that the adaptation of plantation slavery was a gradual process and was the major reason for the factionalism among the tribe. Richard Halliburton, Jr., *Red Over Black: Slavery Among the Cherokee Indians* (Westport, Conn.: Greenwood Press, 1976), concludes that slavery among the Cherokees was virtually identical to slavery among southern whites and that Indians did not always treat their slaves better than whites did.

Ron Satz, *American Indian Policy in the Jacksonian Era* (Lincoln: University of Nebraska Press, 1975), gives a balanced account of government policies and the problems involved in Indian removal. Michael Paul Rogin, *Fathers and Children: Andrew Jackson and the Subjugation of the American Indian* (New York: Alfred A. Knopf, 1975), is a psychological study arguing that as a result of an early separation from his parents, Jackson was an anxiety victim who sought to prove his manhood through the destruction of the Indians. A more favorable view of Jackson may be found in Francis Paul Prucha, "Andrew Jackson's Indian Policy: A Reassessment," *Journal of American History* 56 (December 1969): 527–39.

For the most comprehensive treatment of governmental Indian policy, one should consult the monumental work by Prucha, *The Great Father: The United States Government and the American Indian*, 2 vols. (Lincoln: University of Nebraska Press, 1984). That the seeds of removal originated in Jeffersonian policy is argued by Bernard W. Sheehan, *Seeds of Extinction: Jeffersonian Philanthropy and the American Indian* (Chapel Hill: University of North Carolina Press, 1973). Now dated but still valuable is the work that sets the tone for much of the later writing on removal: Annie H. Abel, "The History of Events Resulting in Indian Consolidation West of the Mississippi," *Annual Report of the American Historical Association for the Year 1906*, 2 vols. (Washington, D.C.: Government Printing Office, 1908), 1:233–450. Two other more recent works in the same vein are Samuel Carter III, *Cherokee Sunset, A Nation Betrayed: A Narrative of Travail and Triumph, Persecution and Exile* (Garden City, N.Y.: Doubleday, 1976), and Dale Van Every, *Disinherited: The Lost Birthright of the American Indian* (New York: William Morrow, 1966).

The most complete bibliography of removal can be found in Howard L. Meredith, *Cherokee Removal: An Historiographic Report* (Oklahoma City: Oklahoma Educational Television Authority, c. 1978). The Georgia view of removal is discussed fully by the pro-removal Georgia politician Wilson Lumpkin in his *The Removal of the Cherokee Indians from Georgia*, 2 vols. (New York: Dodd, Mead, 1907), and in a more recent scholarly approach by Carl J. Vipperman, "Forcibly If We Must: The Georgia Case for the Cherokee Removal, 1802–1832," *Journal of Cherokee Studies* 3 (Spring 1978): 104–11. Also helpful are the case studies by Louis Filler and Allen Guttman, *The Removal of the Cherokee Nation: Manifest Destiny or National Dishonor* (Boston: D. C. Heath, 1965). A good analysis of the Supreme Court cases dealing with Cherokee removal is found in Joseph C. Burke, "The Cherokee Cases: A Study in Law, Politics, and Morality," *Stanford Law Review* 21 (February 1969): 500–531; Anton-Hermann Chroust, "Did President Jackson Actually Threaten the Supreme Court with Nonenforcement of Its Injunction Against the State of Georgia?" *American Journal of Legal History* 5 (January 1960): 76–78; and William F. Swindler, "Politics as Law: The Cherokee Cases," *American Indian Law Review* 3 (1975): 7–20. For the relationship between the nullification crisis and Cherokee removal, see Edwin A. Miles, "After John Marshall's Decision: Worcester v. Georgia and the Nullification Crisis," *Journal of Southern History* 39 (November 1973): 519–44.

The Cherokee view of removal is perhaps best stated in their newspaper, the *Cherokee Phoenix*. The writings of one of the chief white defenders of the Cherokee cause are found in *Cherokee Removal: The "William Penn" Essays and Other Writings of Jeremiah Evarts*, ed. Francis Paul Prucha (Knoxville: University of Tennessee Press, 1981). Evarts was the secretary of the

American Board of Commissioners for Foreign Missions. The best and most recent biography of the Cherokee chief who more than any individual sought to avoid removal is Gary E. Moulton, *John Ross: Cherokee Chief* (Athens: University of Georgia Press, 1978). Moulton has recently edited Ross's papers, which allows one more insight into the public and private life of the "ablest political figure of Cherokee history." See *The Papers of Chief John Ross*, ed. Gary E. Moulton, 2 vols. (Norman: University of Oklahoma Press, 1985), 3. For a brief but well-researched look at Ross's efforts to stop removal, see Walter H. Conser, Jr., "John Ross and the Cherokee Resistance Campaign," *Journal of Southern History* 44 (May 1978): 191–212. These works might be balanced with the story of Ross's political opponents or of the treaty party led by Major Ridge, John Ridge, and Elias Boudinot. These individuals are covered in Thurman Wilkins's well-researched and sympathetic *Cherokee Tragedy: The Ridge Family and the Decimation of a People*, 2d ed., rev. (Norman: University of Oklahoma Press, 1986), and in the standard biography of Boudinot by Ralph H. Gabriel, *Elias Boudinot, Cherokee, and His America* (Norman: University of Oklahoma Press, 1941). The writings of the treaty party can be examined in *Cherokee Cavaliers: Forty Years of Cherokee History as Told in the Correspondence of the Ridge-Watie-Boudinot Family*, ed. Edward E. Dale and Gaston Litton (Norman: University of Oklahoma Press, 1939), and *Cherokee Editor: The Writings of Elias Boudinot*, ed. Theda Perdue (Knoxville: University of Tennessee Press, 1983).

The details of the actual removal and the events immediately preceding it can be found in Grant Foreman, *Indian Removal: The Emigration of the Five Civilized Tribes of Indians*, rev. ed., with a foreword by Angie Debo (Norman: University of Oklahoma Press, 1986); Jesse Burt and Robert B. Ferguson, *The Removal of the Cherokee Indians from Georgia* (Nashville: Abingdon Press, 1973); and Robert C. White, *Cherokee Indian Removal from the Lower Hiwassee Valley* (Cleveland, Tenn.: Cleveland State Community College, 1973). For shorter and more scholarly versions of these events, see Kenneth Penn Davis, "The Cherokee Removal, 1835–1838," *Tennessee Historical Quarterly* 32 (Winter 1975): 311–30; Ronald N. Satz, "Cherokee Traditionalism, Protestant Evangelism, and the Trail of Tears," *Tennessee Historical Quarterly* 44 (Fall, Winter 1985): 285–301, 380–401; James Franklin Corn, "Removal of the Cherokee Indians from the East," *Filson*

Club Historical Quarterly 27 (1953): 36–51; Donald Grinde, Jr., "Cherokee Removal and American Politics," *Indian Historian* 8 (1975): 33–42, 56; and James R. Christianson, "Removal: A Foundation for the Formation of Federalized Indian Policy," *Journal of Cherokee Studies* 10 (Fall 1985): 215–29. For the role and view of Cherokee women in removal, see Theda Perdue, "Cherokee Women and the Trail of Tears," *Journal of Women's History* 1 (Spring 1989): 14–30. Some interesting primary materials on Cherokee removal by both whites and Cherokees are collected in Duane H. King and E. Raymond Evans, eds., "The Trail of Tears: Primary Documents on the Cherokee Removal," *Journal of Cherokee Studies* 3 (Summer 1978). A special issue of the *Georgia Historical Quarterly*, vol. 73 (Fall 1989), has also been dedicated to the Trail of Tears.

Without a doubt the best work dealing with the problems and factionalism that existed among the Cherokee in the West after removal is Morris L. Wardell, *A Political History of the Cherokee Nation, 1838–1907* (Reprint, Norman: University of Oklahoma Press, 1977). The reprint contains a very useful updated bibliographical essay by Rennard Strickland. Also helpful are Grant Foreman, *The Five Civilized Tribes*, rev. ed. (Norman: University of Oklahoma Press, 1953); Brad Agnew, *Fort Gibson: Terminal on the Trail of Tears* (Norman: University of Oklahoma Press, 1980); and Gerard Reed, "Postremoval Factionalism in the Cherokee Nation," in *Cherokee Indian Nation*, ed. King, 148–63. A thousand or so Cherokees escaped removal and remained in the mountains of North Carolina. This escape was due partially to an earlier treaty (1819) with the United States that allowed Cherokees residing in areas ceded by that treaty to remain and to apply for citizenship. Although the Cherokee hero Tsali was not responsible for the survival of the Eastern Band, his role was critical to the non-removal of a number of Cherokees. These ideas and others are interestingly explored in John R. Finger, *The Eastern Band of Cherokees, 1819–1900* (Knoxville: University of Tennessee Press, 1984).

Contributors

WILLIAM L. ANDERSON is a professor of history at Western Carolina University. He is the coauthor with James A. Lewis of *A Guide to Cherokee Documents in Foreign Archives* and has published articles on the Cherokees in *Georgia Historical Quarterly, Journal of Cherokee Studies, Native Press Research Journal,* and the *North Carolina Historical Review.* He is a member of the editorial board of the *Journal of Cherokee Studies* and of the advisory board of the Museum of the Cherokee Indian.

JOHN R. FINGER is a professor of history at the University of Tennessee at Knoxville. He is the author of *The Eastern Band of Cherokees, 1819–1900,* as well as numerous articles on Cherokees and the American frontier that have appeared in such journals as *Journal of Cherokee Studies, Journal of Southern History,* and the *North Carolina Historical Review.* He has recently completed his second book on the Eastern Band, tentatively titled "Cherokee Americans: The Eastern Band of Cherokees in the Twentieth Century."

THEDA PERDUE is a professor of history at the University of Kentucky. She is the author of *Slavery and the Evolution of Cherokee Society, 1540–1866, Native Carolinians: The Indians of North Carolina,* and *The Cherokee* as well as the editor of *Nations Remembered: An Oral History of the Five Civilized Tribes, 1865–1907* and *Cherokee Editor: The Writings of Elias Boudinot.* She is currently working on a monograph entitled "Cherokee Women: A Study in Changing Roles."

RONALD N. SATZ is dean of graduate studies, director of research, and a professor of history at the University of Wisconsin at Eau Claire. In addition to numerous articles and book reviews, his published works include *American Indian Policy in the Jacksonian Era* and *Tennessee's Indian Peoples: From White Contact to Removal.* He has also served as a consultant to the Native American Rights Fund and as a member of the editorial advisory board of the *American Indian Quarterly.*

RENNARD STRICKLAND is director of the American Indian Law and Policy Center at the University of Oklahoma. He has written and edited numerous books on the Cherokee and Oklahoma Indians, including *Fire and the Spirits: Cherokee Law from Clan to Court* (coauthor with Earl Boyd Pierce), *Starr's History of the Cherokees* (coeditor with Jack Gregory), and *Oklahoma Memories* (coeditor with Ann H. Morgan).

WILLIAM M. STRICKLAND was the acting head of the Department of Speech and Theatre Arts at the University of South Carolina at Columbia at the time of his death. His dissertation was on the rhetoric of Cherokee removal from Georgia, 1828–32 (Louisiana State University, 1975). He had published articles on the Cherokee in the *Journal of Cherokee Studies* and *Southern Speech Communication Journal*.

RUSSELL THORNTON is a professor of sociology at the University of California at Berkeley. He is the author of *Sociology of American Indians: A Critical Bibliography* (with Mary Grasmick), *We Shall Live Again: The 1870 and 1890 Ghost Dance Movement as Demographic Revitalization*, and *American Indian Holocaust and Survival: A Population History Since 1492*. Thornton has recently completed a demographic history of the Cherokees.

DOUGLAS C. WILMS is a professor of geography at the University of North Carolina at Wilmington. His dissertation was on Cherokee land use in Georgia, 1800–1838 (University of Georgia, 1972). He has published numerous articles on the Cherokees in such journals as *Chronicles of Oklahoma*, *Appalachian Journal*, *Journal of Cherokee Studies*, and *Southwestern Geographer*.

Index

Index

Dale, Edward E., 137 (n. 23)
Dawes Act (1887), 122
Dawes Commission, 123–24, 126, 128
Deacon, Reuben, 102
Debo, Angie, 126
Department of Interior, 76
Dick, Cecil (Cherokee), 131
Distribution Act (1962), 128
Downing Party, 119
Drowning Bear (Cherokee), 97–98, 100, 105
Dudley, Edward, 101–2

Eastern Band of Cherokees. *See* Cherokee Indians: Eastern Band of
Easton, John, 56
Etowah (Cherokee district), 60
Etowah River, 16
Evans, J.P., 60

Farb, Peter, 47 (n. 13)
Featherstonhaugh, George, 43
Five Civilized Tribes, 83, 117, 118, 121–22, 124. *See also* Cherokee Indians; Chickasaw Indians; Choctaw Indians; Creek Indians; Seminole Indians
Foreman, Grant, 84, 126
Fort Butler (N.C.), 102
Fort Delaney (N.C.), 102
Fort Gibson (Okla.), 114
Fort Hembrie (N.C.), 102
Fort Lindsay (N.C.), 102
Fort Loudoun (Tenn.), 57
Fort Smith (Ark.), 117, 129
Foster, James, 70
Frelinghuyson, Theodore, 30
French and Indian War, 70

Fritz, Henry, 42

Georgia, xii, xiii, 1–24, 55, 66, 67, 68, 96, 106, 113
Georgia Compact of 1802, xi
General Allotment Act, 122
Gilmer, George, 55–56
"Golden Age of the Cherokee," 114
Great Society programs, 130
Gunter, Edward (Cherokee), 74 (n. 24)
Gunter, John (Cherokee), 69

Hall, Edward T., 36, 44
Handlin, Oscar, 36, 44
Harrison, Benjamin, 122
Hastings, William Wirt (Cherokee), 127
Haweis (Cherokee town), 9
Henderson Roll of 1835. *See* Cherokee Indians: population and censuses
Hermitage, 29
Hiwassee River, 80, 97, 105
Hog Bite (Cherokee), 103
Honey Springs, Battle of, 116
Horseshoe Bend, Battle of, 107
Howard, R. Palmer, 84

Illinois, 80, 92
Illinois River, 78
Indian Appropriations Act (1889), 121
Indian Civil Rights Act, 131
Indian Claims Commission (1946), 128
Indian Reorganization Act, xiii
Indian Reservation Economies, 130
Indian Territory, 80–84, 119, 120, 121. *See also* Oklahoma
Indiana, 92

Index

Index